Flying the Pacific Northwest

11-21-2013

Copyright © 2013 Wayne J. Lutz

All rights reserved. No part of this publication may be reproduced, stored in a retrieval system, or transmitted, in any form or by any means, electronic, mechanical, photocopying, recording, or otherwise, without the written prior permission of the author. Reviewers are authorized to quote short passages within a book review, as permitted under the United States Copyright Act of 1976.

Note for Librarians: a catalog record for this book that includes Dewey Decimal Classification and U.S. Library of Congress numbers is available from the Library and Archives of Canada. The complete catalog record can be obtained from their online database at:
www.collectionscanada.ca/amicus/index-e.html

ISBN 978-1-927438-13-8
Printed in the United States of America

Powell River Books
Powell RIver, BC

Book sales online at:
www.powellriverbooks.com
phone: 604-483-1704
email: wlutz@mtsac.edu

10 9 8 7 6 5 4 3 2 1

Flying the Pacific Northwest

Wayne J. Lutz

2013
Powell River Books

To my incredible copilot...

George, too

The stories are true, and the characters are real. Some details are adjusted to protect the guilty. All of the mistakes rest solidly with the author.

The author is a certified flight instructor who strives to present material in accordance with FAA-approved procedures. However, much of the material contained in this book involves personal techniques, navigational data that may be outdated, and individual recommendations that could prove hazardous to the operation of an aircraft. The author and publisher take no responsibility for the currency and accuracy of any of the methods or materials described in this book.

Front Cover Photo:
Siletz Bay Airport at GlenEden Beach, Oregon

Books by Wayne J. Lutz

Costal British Columbia Stories
Up the Lake
Up the Main
Up the Winter Trail
Up the Strait
Up the Airway
Farther Up the Lake
Farther Up the Main
Farther Up the Strait
Cabin Number 5
Off the Grid
Up the Inlet

Science Fiction Titles
Echo of a Distant Planet
Inbound to Earth
Anomaly at Fortune Lake
When Galaxies Collide
Across the Galactic Sea

Paccific Northwest Series
FLying the Pacific Northwest
Paddling the Pacific Northwest

www.PowellRiverBooks.com

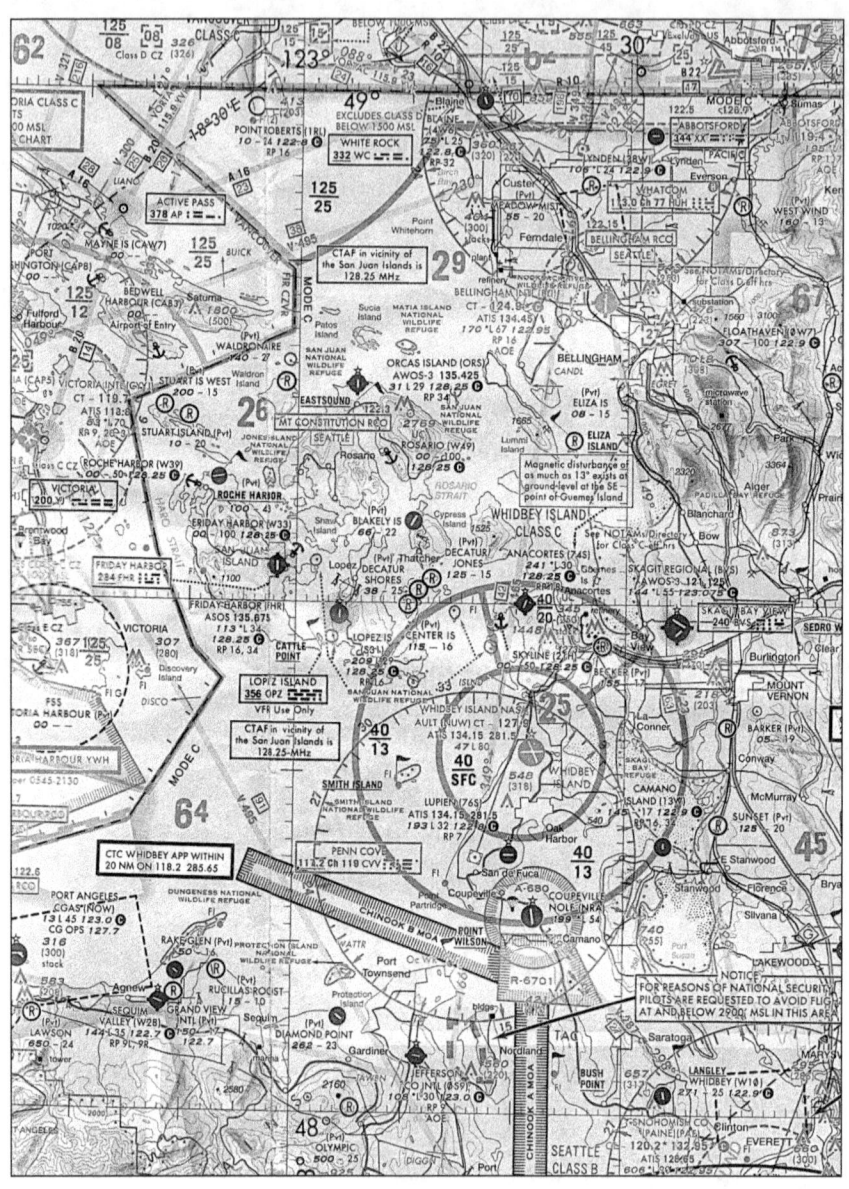

Local flying area – Bellingham, Washington

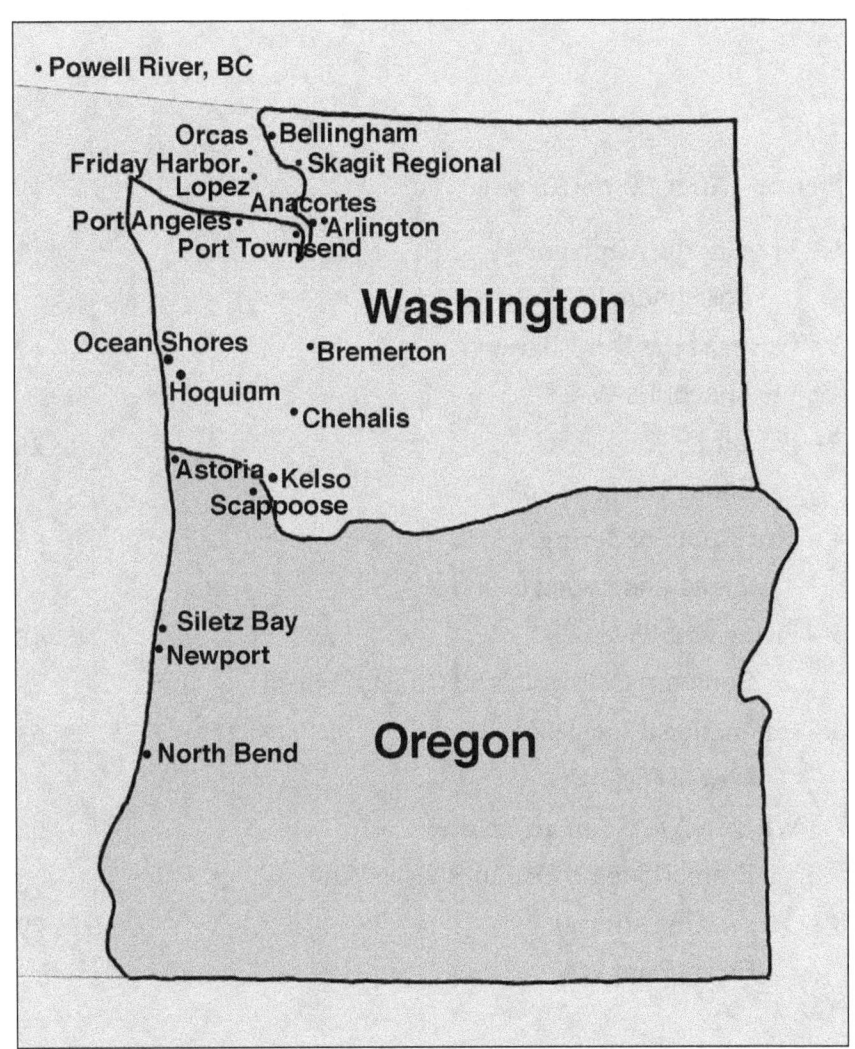

Airports featured in *Flying the Pacific Northwest*

Contents

Preface – After *Up the Airway* 10

1 – I've Got the Airplane 12
    Bellingham WA

2 – Omen of the Dead Battery 17
    Anacortes WA

3 – Big Bird 26
    Friday Harbour WA

4 – First Robin of Spring 35
    Orcas and Lopez Island WA

5 – Flying with Fred 48
    Southern California and Coastal British Columbia

6 – International Incident 63
    Powell River BC

7 – Why Are We Going to Seattle? 66
    Bremerton and Ocean Shores WA

8 – Heads-Up (Always) 79
    Bellingham WA

CENTER-OF-BOOK ILLUSTRATIONS	87
9 – Rented Cop Cars	92
Newport OR	
10 – Airport Misguides	99
Scappoose OR and Chehalis-Centralia WA	
11 – Experimental Mecca and Oil Dipsticks	111
Arlington WA	
12 – South on Victor 27	121
Washington, Oregon, and California	
13 – Renewal	131
Burlington-Skagit Regional and Port Angeles WA	
14– Why Favorites are Favorites	140
Siletz Bay OR and Chealis WA	
About the Author	148
Appendix A – Cockpit Instruments and Avionics	150
Appendix B – Aviation Terminology and Abbreviations . . .	165
Appendix C – Airport Index	169

Preface

After *Up the Airway*

LIFE CHANGES, AND THINGS THAT WERE once important fade with time. But addiction to flying lasts forever.

When I wrote *Up the Airway* for the series entitled *Coastal British Columbia Stories*, it was easy to envision a follow-up volume. But I wouldn't have guessed the sequel would involve flying in the United States. My trusty Piper Arrow had moved to Canada, and she was happy there. Well, as happy as an airplane can be in a colder, wetter climate – parked in an open-ended hangar. There were other extenuating circumstances, as well, including a home airport with dwindling maintenance support and soon-to-be lack of fuel facilities. Plus, N41997 was a U.S. airplane, registered in the States and flown by two FAA-licensed pilots. Still, I would have guessed that my increasing ties to Canada would lead to a permanent Canadian home for the Arrow as well. But it wasn't to be.

When all of the legal wrangling was complete (coupled with the realities of dwindling fuel and maintenance resources at my Canadian airport), N41997 moved back home to Bellingham, Washington. But that raised a new opportunity – exploration of the beautiful Pacific Northwest by air during those periods when I returned to the States. With the Arrow waiting for me when I came back to Bellingham (quite regularly), it was an added incentive to occasionally leave my beloved cabin in Canada. It takes a lot to draw me away from my floating home on BC's Powell Lake.

Thus, the concept for this book was born, with plenty of excuses for flying. This was also a time when the Arrow had been sitting idle way too much. I was slipping away from flight proficiency; a discouraging feeling that eventually catches up with many pilots. As the reader will notice, the challenge of deteriorating flight currency is a recurring theme. This publication is proof that pilots can solve that dilemma, and it doesn't take writing a book to acquire the cure.

The hundred-dollar hamburger has always been an inside joke among aviators. We often need an excuse to fly, and lunch at an airport cafe is one solution. With today's fuel prices, it should be called the three-hundred-dollar hamburger. But how do you value the greatest things in life? For pilots, it's impossible to put a price tag on the wonders of flight. Excuses or no excuses, we must fly.

For pilots, I offer an inside look into what makes us tick. Both our flying skills and our aviation psyche are explored in this book. If you want to find reasons to fly, you'll find them here. Better yet, maybe you'll discover that excuses are not needed. Just flying around the flagpole (your local traffic pattern) is often worth the effort, even if it takes 3 hours to log 30 minutes.

For non-pilots, I accept a special challenge. To experience the thrill of flight, you don't need to learn to fly. You can take control of a Piper Arrow in these pages. As your flight instructor, I'll be your guide. Throughout this book, I've worked hard at drawing the aviation enthusiast into my world of flying.

Whether you're a ten-thousand-hour pilot or an armchair adventurist, all are welcome aboard. Climb into the left seat, reach forward – take the yoke in your left hand, and the throttle in your right. Hold your feet on the brakes, and then push the throttle forward. Release the brakes – you've been cleared for takeoff. I'll be sitting in the right seat beside you, cheering you on, each and every mile along the airway.

Chapter 1

I've Got the Airplane
Bellingham WA

"We need to fly more often," says Margy as we climb through seven hundred feet, southbound out of Bellingham, Washington.

"Not a good day," I reply.

Our lack of currency in this airplane has surfaced several times in the last few minutes. When you don't fly regularly, it shows. So far we've demonstrated amateur airmanship twice in the last fifteen minutes, and we're barely airborne.

"Niner-Niner-Seven, contact Victoria Terminal," instructs Bellingham Tower.

This is normal procedure. Victoria's frequency is already set in the flip-flop window of our communications radio, because we were expecting it. It's part of the IFR Kieno Departure procedure. I'm comfortable with the world of instrument flight rules. The radio work comes back automatically after my six weeks absence from flying. Not so the more basic stuff – like taxiing. What happened to us a few minutes ago on the ground at Bellingham was inexcusable.

"Roger, switching to Terminal," I reply.

I push the button that brings the preset frequency into position.

"Victoria Terminal, November Four-One-Niner-Niner-Seven, out of one thousand two hundred for five thousand."

I'm relaxed now, back in the groove. Talking on the radio tends to settle me down. The structure of the IFR world provides a calming influence.

"Four-One-Niner-Niner-Seven, Victoria. I have you as a primary target, but your transponder appears to be inop," says the professional voice on the Canadian frequency.

Oh, that's because we forgot to turn it on. So that's the third error in the first five miles. Two experienced pilots, and neither notices the transponder is still in *Standby* mode.

"Roger, let me try recycling it," I reply.

Air traffic controllers probably hear this too often to be fooled by the real facts.

"Niner-Niner-Seven, I've got your Mode-C now," replies the controller, not questioning my little white lie. "Radar identified, five southwest of Bellingham. Altitude readout is one thousand four hundred."

"Nine-Nine-Seven concurs with the altitude. Thank you."

Without punching the microphone button, I speak to Margy over our intercom's hot mike.

"Like you said, we need to fly more often."

"Roger that," replies Margy.

* * * * *

WHAT HAPPENED ON THE GROUND back at Bellingham was more than embarrassing. It was downright ridiculous.

When we fly, Margy traditionally starts the engine and usually taxis the airplane. This gives me time to set up the radios, copy the instrument clearance (we seldom fly under visual flight rules), and prepare the navigation radios for the departure route. Margy also performs most of the takeoffs, allowing me the opportunity to closely monitor the engine gauges during the departure and make the radio calls. It's a cockpit management routine that works well for both of us.

On this particular morning, the airplane has sat inactive for six weeks. Thus, it will be important to catch the firing of the engine immediately and properly set the throttle for warm-up before too many blades of the prop swing past the top of the cowling. Otherwise, the battery may not survive long enough to get us going. This is an area of expertise for Margy, and she almost always catches the start process by the third or fourth blade. Today is no exception.

"Oil pressure green," says Margy, as soon as the engine is running. "Throttle seems stiff."

I watch her move the throttle slowly forward and back. From my seat on the right side of the airplane, the throttle movement appears jerky, and I hear the engine surge.

"Let me check it," I say. "I've got the airplane."

With two pilots, it's always important to know who's in charge of the airplane at any particular moment. More than a few accidents have occurred due to lack of clarity regarding who's in control.

"You've got it," replies Margy, using the traditional response for this situation.

Now my feet are on the brakes (the top of the rudder pedals), and my left hand is on the throttle. I move the throttle slowly back and forth until I'm satisfied this is merely a stiffness resulting from over a month of inactivity.

"Seems fine now," I say. "Probably just stiff from sitting around…"

A bad noise interrupts me – a shrill squeal in the intercom just before it goes suddenly dead. Simultaneously, the brightly colored moving map in front of us goes blank. Total electrical failure.

"Oh!" I yell. "I forgot to turn on the alternator."

We've been on battery power since we started the engine, and it was my job to turn on the alternator. But there the red switch sits, still toggled off. With an already low battery from weeks of inactivity, we managed to start the engine only through Margy's proven expertise in catching the third blade. But it doesn't take long to deplete the battery while we sit here playing with the throttle. I flip the red switch to the "on" position, and the intercom and moving map come back to life instantly.

"Sorry," I say. "We need to fly more often."

It's not much of an excuse, but a good reminder to be careful today. Anything could happen. Turning on the alternator is normally so automatic it's hard to believe I could miss this simple step.

With the electrical system back to normal, I return to getting my tasks complete, which includes copying our IFR clearance to Port Townsend. Meanwhile, we've been assigned taxi instructions to Runway Three-Four, so this means straight ahead to the parallel taxiway, and then a left turn to the run-up area.

I've been holding the brakes since I took control of the airplane to check the throttle, so now I release the pedals and relinquish control to Margy. As usual, she'll taxi the airplane to the assigned runway.

As soon as I let up on the brakes, the Piper Arrow moves slowly ahead, not needing any additional throttle to taxi. In another hundred feet, we'll turn left towards the approach end of Runway Three-Four. But as we approach the parallel taxiway, Margy doesn't lead the turn as she normally does.

We creep past where she would typically begin pushing the left rudder pedal (linked to the nose wheel steering), but I hesitate to intervene. It's certainly not critical, since there's still time to make the turn, but her lack of currency in this airplane is showing. She should turn – now!

"I've got it!" I yell, as I ram my foot on the left rudder pedal, adding pressure to the top of the pedal to assure the brake helps us pivot to the left.

Then I realize what has happened.

"I thought you had the airplane," I say to Margy.

"I thought you had it," she replies.

It wouldn't have been a fatal accident, but we could have done some damage if we rolled off the taxiway. This airplane taxis in a straight line with little need of attention – so well, in fact, that neither of us knew no one was in charge.

I can see the accident report now: "The Piper Arrow departed the pavement, the rotating propeller hit a taxiway light, and complete engine teardown was necessitated to assure the crankshaft wasn't damaged. Investigation reveals no one was taxiing the airplane at the time of accident."

* * * * *

THE REST OF THE FLIGHT to Port Townsend goes well. This trip serves as a reminder that we need to fly more often. Like many pilots in similar situations, we resolve to spend more time in the air. But we don't.

Since the purchase of the Piper Arrow twenty years ago, Margy and I have typically flown 200 hours per year, a respectable record for a private aircraft. But in recent years, with our time now split between the U.S. and Canada, we fly a lot less. This year (2008) has been the worst on record. We're struggling for fifty hours, and that's poor utilization of a plane like this.

For us, flying is one of life's greatest pleasures, so we need to get back on track. The Arrow is now based in Bellingham, and we resolve to fly it every time we return to the States. But that's not as easy as it sounds.

Left base leg, Bellingham International Airport, Washington

Chapter 2

Omen of the Dead Battery
Anacortes WA

During a cloudy day in May, we plan to end our last of five days in the States with a local flight. We arrive at the airport late in the afternoon, pull the airplane out of the hangar, and hop aboard for a quick trip to Anacortes. This will be a short flight, but enough to get the oil flowing and cylinder temperatures into the green, important considerations for an aircraft that doesn't fly regularly.

When Margy cranks the starter, this time she doesn't get the engine firing on the third blade rotation, or even the fourth. By the fifth blade, with the propeller barely rotating, the battery is dead. The airplane has sat too long, and today is a lost cause. Tomorrow we're scheduled for the morning ferry up the British Columbia coast. By the time we return to the States again, our Arrow will have been idle without a flight for over two months. And now it will remain here even longer with a dead battery.

"Let's sell the damn thing," I say, as Margy tries one last time to get the engine going.

The prop doesn't even rotate this time. The battery is totally discharged, and I'm grumped. When I get frustrated, like any red-blooded American boy, I say things I don't mean. Margy has heard this rant before.

"Okay," she says. "But all we really need to do is to fly more often, and then this wouldn't happen."

True, but easier said than done. As always, I cool off quickly, and then I'm willing to listen when Margy makes a suggestion.

"Why don't we go to a store and buy a battery charger, right now," she says. "We need one here in the hangar anyway, with most of our time spent in Canada. The battery can charge tonight, and we can go flying tomorrow. Can't we delay going north for one more day?"

The answer is obvious. We have time on our hands. But the problem with her suggestion is the whole concept of going "home." Finally, after decades of being visitors to Canada, we've recently become permanent residents. That means our "home" truly is in Canada, and we love it there. To not go home on schedule would be difficult. Then again, I envision our Piper Arrow sitting another full month without flying. It will be bad for the airplane and bad for us.

So we go to an automotive store, and I buy a trickle charger and multimeter to determine the battery's condition. It seems obvious that the battery is dead today, but there could be more to the situation than meets the eye. Later in the afternoon, we're back in the hangar, where I check the battery voltage – 11.85, too low to crank the airplane's starter. I hook up the battery charger, make sure the amber *Charging* light is illuminated, and lock up the hangar for the night.

Piper Arrow N41997 in Bellingham hangar

*****

DAWN THE NEXT DAY SHINES BRIGHT, both physically and psychologically. Although it was a tough decision to delay our trip home, the sky is clear, and it's a perfect day to fly. Besides, while pondering our dilemma regarding how to get airborne more often, I've come up with a rationalized solution. I'm now an established author, with five books to my credit. All of these volumes are in a series entitled *Coastal British Columbia Stories*, and the most recent Canadian book is about flying the BC coast (*Up the Airway*, Powell River Books, 2008). But who's to say I can't write a book about flying in the United States. I've got lots of experience as a flight instructor, and writing another book about flying would provide me with incentive to use the Piper Arrow as a research tool. It's such an obvious solution; I'm amazed I haven't considered it.

Even before I arrive at the airport, I'm compiling a mental list of places we could visit to get started writing the book you are now reading: *Flying the Pacific Northwest*.

My disposition has changed for the better, but when I open the hangar door, there's an immediate setback. The amber *Charging* light is no longer illuminated, nor is the green *Charged* light. What has gone wrong?

It doesn't take long to determine the problem. When I connected charger the day before, I added it to the set of cords keeping the Arrow warm and dry. One cord leads to a 60-watt bulb that heats the cockpit and keeps avionics moisture under control. Another cord goes to an exhaust pipe heating element that (in accordance with my personal theory) assists in keeping the engine block warm, which helps control acidic moisture buildup in the crankcase. It's a bit of overkill for an airplane stored inside, but unheated hangars in the Pacific Northwest are cold and damp most of the year.

Of course, my electrical setup is considerate of energy consumption, with a timer operating these heating accessories only a few hours per day. My battery charger, tied into this electrical connection, was also on the timer. So rather than charging the battery for almost a full day, I've added electrons for only a few hours.

The multimeter registers 12.3 volts, a respectable charge, but maybe not enough to get the engine started. This will take a masterful pilot at the controls, and Margy nervously accepts the challenge.

During her pre-start checklist, she detects a popped circuit breaker, which is another psychological setback. But it probably isn't as bad as it appears.

"Fuel pump," says Margy, as she identifies the popped breaker.

"Let's reset it and see what happens," I reply.

A circuit breaker can be an indicator of important problems. But today the likely explanation is the previous aborted start. When a drained battery struggles to crank an airplane engine, with the electric fuel pump activated (as is standard during starts), it wouldn't be uncommon to pop the pump's breaker.

During today's start-up cycle, Margy gets a clean start, with plenty of cranking power to spare. As soon as the engine is running, with the throttle established at idle, Margy notes another problem.

"Trim light," she says over the intercom. "But the fuel pump seems okay."

The red trim light is part of the flight director system, warning us the automatic self-test of the autopilot trim isn't happy. A flight director is unusual for a Piper Arrow, an avionics subsystem usually reserved for airliners. But we use this sophisticated autopilot efficiently, and it adds considerable luxury on cross-country flights. It also assists us with precise maneuvering. The trim light tends to come on when there's an electrical anomaly, and certainly there have been lots of those in the last 24 hours.

"Who has the airplane?" jokes Margy, as we roll forward towards the parallel taxiway.

"You do," I reply. "And don't forget it."

While Margy taxis to Runway Three-Four, I have little to do but absorb our surroundings. This will be a visual flight rules trip, relatively rare for us. The GPS is set to *Direct Anacortes*, and it's about all we'll need as far as the avionics panel is concerned.

In the past few years, I've developed a comfortable familiarity with Bellingham Airport. This is our common entry and departure point for Canada. As an international airport for private and corporate aircraft, Bellingham has a good mix of flight activity, but it never seems to get too busy for the capabilities of the single north-south runway. It's a simple airport layout with a control tower staff that's generally relaxed, yet professional.

Pilots visiting here, however, will need a rental car or a taxicab to get to the local sights. The small cafe in the terminal is snacks only, with no restaurants within easy walking distance (soon to change, with a new on-airport hotel scheduled for 2014). The biggest nearby attraction is Bellis Fair Mall, a big shopping center that's barely within hiking distance (2 miles). The harbor is a major port for recreational boats, with a significant commercial fishing fleet. It's well beyond walking distance, but visitors will find it worth a trip by taxi. Walking around the harbor on the picturesque trail can easily fill a lazy summer afternoon, taking you past a hotel, several restaurants, and a variety of marine stores.

Today, ground control instructs us to follow an Allegiant Air MD-83 to the runway, the only other aircraft on the frequency. As we taxi, Margy provides more evidence that we're still fumbling with our bout of flight inactivity.

"I forgot my cell phone," she says. "Do you have yours?"

"No. We need to get our act together."

"Do we have the hand-held radio?"

"I forgot that, too."

This will be only a short journey on a clear day, but leaving our phones and emergency VHF radio behind isn't a good start. We aren't as smoothly coordinated in our preparation for flight as we normally are. Margy and I work well together in the cockpit as a team. We watch each other's actions closely, a superb safety feature. But already today, there's a lot to watch. And we haven't even left the ground.

As we taxi, I pull out the Seattle Sectional from my flight bag. It's two years out of date, an indicator of how seldom we fly under visual flight rules. My IFR charts are current, so we have all the required airspace data needed today, but we'll need a current VFR chart to feel comfortable exploring regional airports during future flights. I look forward to occasionally going back to the basics of VFR after years of point-to-point IFR travel. Under instrument flight routes, airspace is virtually invisible, with air traffic control taking care of the details for the pilot. Turn to a new heading, change frequencies now – overall an easier process than VFR when it comes to airspace.

Cleared for takeoff, Margy taxis onto the runway, sets the brakes, and applies full power, using the Arrow's short-field takeoff procedures, even though Bellingham's runway is plenty long.

"Watch me close," warns Margy.

"Always."

She releases the brakes, and the Arrow accelerates down the runway. Then we're airborne, and all is well again. It often happens like this – sitting on the ground can make you ponder way too many nervous scenarios, which is particularly true when you haven't flown recently. Plus, the process of "getting going" seems like so much effort. But once the engine is running, I always find a sudden sense of relief, and all is okay again. And going airborne brings an almost immediate sensation of calm. As the landing gear retracts upward into the wheel wells, all is <u>really</u> okay. This may sound backwards to non-pilots, but it's a reality to those who fly.

As we climb, with half of the paved surface behind us, Margy retracts the landing gear. Then she reaches down between our seats to move the large lever that withdraws the two notches (20 degrees) of flaps she has set for takeoff. She reduces the black throttle lever to 25 inches of manifold pressure, and pulls back on the blue prop lever to set 2500 rpm. This 25-25 standard is common in airplanes like this with a constant-speed prop. The red mixture control is then reduced to establish 12 gallons per hour for the climb, electric fuel pump off, landing light on (good anti-collision device for birds), and wingtip strobes on (anti-collision for other airplanes). We're on our way!

Meanwhile, I've been closely monitoring the engine gauges, beginning with Margy's first application of power on the runway. I pay close attention to cylinder head temperature. CHT is an important indicator during the climb, and this Arrow has an Alcor four-position gauge that allows me to cycle through all four cylinders. Exhaust gas temperature (EGT) isn't as important at this point in the flight, but I make sure all cylinder EGTs are running at the same level. During the first few minutes of flight, especially after a lengthy period of engine inactivity, I flip from one cylinder to another repeatedly before we leave the airport traffic pattern. All is well with both temperature measurements.

The flight to Anacortes is a quick up-and-down. Short flights are more challenging than long hauls, since everything happens so fast. After only five minutes in level flight at 2500 feet, I ask Margy for the flight controls. She relinquishes the yoke to me with an emphasized: "*You've* got it." We may make mistakes, but we learn from them.

In just a few minutes, I begin the descent, dropping quickly through two thousand feet to make sure we clear the lip of the Class C airspace surrounding Whidbey Island Naval Air Station to the south. Based on the winds at nearby Bellingham and the air-to-air calls of pilots in the pattern at Anacortes, I set up for a downwind entry to Runway Three-Six.

As we slip into the traffic pattern, Margy verifies the windsock is favoring a landing to the north. I report our position to other aircraft on the Unicom frequency, and make the turn to base leg. This is a beautiful runway, recently repaved.

Anacortes, Washington

Anacortes Airport sits majestically on a narrow isthmus of Fidalgo Island, a bit too far from town to walk. But rental cars are readily available for those who want to explore this beautiful area. A nearby tourist attraction well worth the trip (but far beyond walking distance) is Deception Pass, where strong tidal currents flow through the narrow opening between Fidalgo and Whidbey Islands. A visit to Deception Pass leads to a parking lot on the south side of the bridge, where hiking paths wind down to Little North Beach to the west and along the cliffs on the other side of the road. During summer months, passenger tickets for tour boats through the pass can be reserved right at the parking lot. (Details involving this location are available in *Farther Up the Strait*, Chapter 10.)

On the ground at Anacortes Airport, we visit the small terminal for San Juan Airlines. I take a photo of Margy in front of one of their airplanes, a classic 1976 Cessna Turbo 206.

Margy with San Juan Airlines Cessna 206

* * * * *

After a short period exploring the aircraft on the parking ramp at Anacortes, we crank up again, and I align the Arrow on the runway. Usually Margy is quick to relinquish challenging departures to me, and I enjoy an occasional takeoff. This isn't a short field by most standards, but our airplane consumes a lot of pavement when it's full of fuel. I set the flaps for 20-degrees and push the throttle full forward before releasing the brakes. For us, this is our normal departure procedure at most airports. In fact, Margy prefers the feel of the airplane with 20-degrees of flap on all takeoffs, although the flight manual calls for two notches only for short fields.

The climb-out is relaxed, tracking straight north for a few miles to clear the edge of Whidbey's Class C airspace. Then I bank left towards our next stop, Friday Harbor. It seems like a tranquil beginning to my research for a new book. What we don't know at the time is how memorable the next portion of our flight will be. In fact, it warrants a chapter of its own.

Chapter 3

Big Bird
Friday Harbor WA

The flight from Anacortes to Friday Harbor is brief, but I'm immediately comfortable. A few hours earlier, back in Bellingham, I was fighting the aftermath of a dead battery. Only yesterday, I was contemplating selling the airplane. Now I'm feeling the encompassing freedom that flying brings. Often it's like this, a transformation that occurs in the brief time it takes to get airborne and settle down in cruise.

Many of life's adventures provide similar results. If you think about risks too much, as is often the case in advance of taking a leap of any sort, an activity can seem foreboding. The challenge of a trip in a boat into unknown waters, an off-road ride into the wilderness, the first flight after a period of inactivity – once underway, all is well again. Flying fits that mode, since it's so different from the everyday. In a small airplane, you put yourself inside a cramped metal container and burst into the sky at more than two times legal highway speed. What insanity – until you're there again. Then it all settles in, with the magic of flight consuming all of your thoughts. Looking down on the earth from a mile high is a humbling experience. You pass over urban areas where people are struggling for their existence. Meanwhile, up above it all, the world is at peace and seemingly eternal.

Our route takes us over Lopez Island, where we pass just north of the airport. I landed on this runway many years ago; though it deserves another visit soon, next time to include a hike to town. But for now, I bank to the left far enough to allow Margy to snap an aerial photo.

Lopez Airport, Washington

The Unicom at Friday Harbor is bustling with activity, but all is settling down now as an airplane departs the traffic pattern and another reports on final for Runway Three-Four. A Cessna on floats checks in two miles north of the airport, headed for Roche Harbor. I swing the Arrow in a wide turn towards a forty-five degree entry to the established pattern, a right downwind leg for Runway Three-Four.

I reach to my left and move the landing gear lever to the down position, with the normal accompanying airflow noise and the feeling of deceleration. Two quick thumps and the main gear locks in position, a brief pause, and then a mild clunk signifying that the nose wheel is down. I run the GUMPS checklist out loud, a good way to prevent any oversights. Margy backs up each of my actions, just like I watch her operational decisions when she flies.

"*Gas* – on the proper tank, with the pump." (Right tank is fullest, electric fuel pump on.)

"*Undercarriage* – three green."

Right base leg, Friday Harbor Runway 34

"*Mixture* – full rich."

"*Prop* – hold for final."

"*Seatbelts* – secured. Landing checklist complete, except for the prop."

The right turn from base leg aligns us on a one-mile final approach. The wind is nearly right down the runway, perfect conditions.

"Prop forward," I say, pushing the blue lever towards the instrument panel.

We're greeted by the sound of increased engine speed from the prop's decreased angle of pitch. I shade the three gear-down lights with my left hand to assure they are lit. Now my final callout: "Three green with the prop." Out of habit and for safety, I make these verbal calls even when I am alone in the cockpit. It's proven to be a wise personal backup.

Ninety miles per hour, dropping to eighty as we come over the fence. (Our 1974-model Arrow's airspeed indicator is calibrated in MPH rather than knots). With pavement now below us, I begin the flare, holding a nose-high profile as long as possible, pulling back slowly on the yoke to compensate for the decreasing airspeed. *Don't land, don't land*, I say to myself (and sometimes out loud) to extend the flare and assure the nose wheel is off the ground when the main tires hit the pavement.

The touchdown is smooth, as I silently celebrate: *Yeah!* We continue down the runway centerline, bleeding off our speed as we rollout towards the north end, where a right turn takes us to the spacious tie-down area for transient aircraft.

"Friday Harbor Traffic, Arrow Niner-Niner-Seven, clear of the active, to transient parking, Friday Harbor," I report.

Only two other airplanes are parked here. But just as Margy and I are securing the Arrow, the roar of a turbine helicopter approaches from the south. The chopper (on hefty inflatable floats) angles towards the parking area across the ramp from us, settling gracefully into a large paved spot labeled *Twin Engine*. The touchdown is gentle, and the male pilot and his female passenger are out of the helicopter within only a few minutes, walking towards the exit gate at the end of the ramp. Meanwhile, with the turbine engine shut down, the copter's blades still rotate slowly, as the occupants walk away. It's a strange but safe sight for a jet rotorcraft. The turbine engine is off but the rotor is still winding down, unattended.

"Hey, you left your engine running!" I yell to the pilot, as I wave hello.

"Oh, you're right!" he shouts back. "It won't use much fuel while we're gone."

If you can afford your own helicopter to fly to lunch, maybe it isn't such a humorous response. Speaking of fuel, the sign at the automotive gas pumps outside the airport gate get our attention. Car gas is a full 50 cents per gallon more expensive than in nearby Bellingham. Island life has its economic disadvantages.

Our walk to town and the ferry terminal is a nice downhill jaunt. We pass the bicycle shop where we rented bikes last year and toured the island (*Up the Airway*, Chapter 12). Once again, we're here in May, just before the tourist season gets into gear, a nice time for a visit to Friday Harbor.

There are a variety of restaurants to chose from near the ferry terminal, but why argue with success? We've eaten at Downriggers before, and the food and view overlooking the harbor are hard to beat. So we eat a late lunch in the pub, save some of our appetite for an ice cream cone at the shop next door, and then hike back to the airport.

Margy starts the engine and taxis out, using the one-way route to the north end of the runway, where we cross to the parallel taxiway on the other side. This takes us past the small terminal, and towards the run-up area at the approach end of Runway Three-Four. In preparation for the short VFR flight back to Bellingham I have little to do, but Margy will be busy with the pre-takeoff checklist. As we approach the run-up area, she remarks on the small birds flittering in the grass.

"Birds everywhere," she says.

I think about turning on the landing light, a technique that's been documented in some studies as a bird-avoidance procedure. But these are only small birds gathered on the ground. None of them are currently airborne, except for brief flittering from spot to spot beside the runway. Landing lights are "free," but we normally keep ours off until climb-out, when we run our brief post-takeoff checklist. The bulbs seem to last longer when they are kept cool during vibration from the pavement on takeoff roll. A minor decision, or so it seems.

Margy's takeoff checklist complete, she taxis onto the runway as I announce our intensions for a straight-out departure on Unicom frequency. Our plan is to overfly Orcas Island Airport for an aerial photo, and then back to Bellingham.

We're airborne quickly in the slight headwind, traveling light for a change. Under Margy's guidance, the Arrow climbs gracefully through 500 feet, preparing to clear the traffic pattern. She goes through the climb checklist – landing gear and flaps retracted; throttle set at 25-inches; prop at 2500 rpm; mixture set for 12 gallons per hour on the fuel flow meter; electric fuel pump off; landing light and wingtip strobes on.

"A slight right turn, about twenty degrees," I request as we climb through 1000 feet. "That will take us towards Orcas so we can get a picture."

"Look out!" yells Margy.

All I can do is "look." It happens that fast. A seagull, closing with us from nearly straight ahead, zooms past in an instant, just to the right side of the windshield. That's my side of the airplane, and the big bird comes within inches of the prop and windshield. Instantly, the seagull seems to get caught in the slipstream near the fuselage, and rushes rearward.

Bam! It's a subdued whack that doesn't sound too bad, considering the size of this bird. We're climbing at 110 miles per hour, and a seagull in cruise must be doing over 20 mph, so our closing speed exceeds 130. Missing the prop and windshield is a lucky break. Maybe we dodged the bullet completely. So much for landing lights, or maybe that's exactly what saved us.

"Flight controls feel okay," reports Margy, the pitch of her voice noticeably higher than normal. "Do you want me to do anything special?"

"No, just keep climbing for now, while we try to figure out what happened."

Maybe the sound was more of an air pressure whack than anything else. If we're lucky, our slipstream pushed the bird mostly clear of the fuselage and tail.

"That was quite an impact!" says Margy.

"Yes, but not as loud as I would have expected. It sounded like it hit near the baggage door."

I'm looking rearward now, my head turned to the right, and Margy is concentrating on flying the airplane. I twist around in my seat but see no bird guts on the side windows or the baggage door. It's difficult to see much from where I sit.

"How about taking the airplane?" says Margy, her voice almost back to normal. "The controls feel okay, but kind of different."

When I take the yoke, the wheel's control pressures feel normal, and so do the rudder pedals. But there's a faint vibration in the yoke that isn't ordinary. I can hear more than feel a difference in the airplane. It sounds like a mild resonance that makes me suspicious of the engine and prop, although I'm fairly sure they were clear of the impact zone. I scan through all four cylinders with the CHT and EGT gauge. The temperature indications look normal.

"My god!" gasps Margy. "Look at the tail!"

She's looking behind me on my side of the airplane, focused on the horizontal stabilator. For some reason, I didn't notice what she now sees when I first looked rearward. When I glance over my shoulder this time, the damage is immediately evident. A wide red blob and a big dent on the stabilator's outboard section look ominous.

"Big bird," I say, trying to make light of the situation.

"Straight to Bellingham?" she suggests.

"Should be only 30 more degrees to the right," I reply.

We're still climbing, and the aircraft is tracking straight, but 30 degrees may be a big turn under conditions like these. I ease the yoke to the right, and the airplane responds normally, but still there's that background vibration.

"Get a photo of Orcas," I say, noticing the airport is nearly below Margy's side of the airplane.

"Not now!" she says. "I'm a bit worried."

"Okay. I'll level off here. It's only a few minutes to Bellingham."

It's obvious that Bellingham Airport is our best destination. It's only twenty nautical miles in front of us, with full maintenance facilities (which we'll need). Besides, the airport has complete emergency services, a benefit of being served by Horizon and Allegiant Airlines. Orcas Airport will remain within gliding distance for another five miles, making it an ideal alternate if the situation deteriorates.

I tune in the ATIS frequency for Bellingham's weather, and simultaneously dial up the control tower on the other radio. The tower is busier than I had hoped. One airplane is a few miles to the northwest, with instructions from the tower to enter a left downwind for Runway Three-Four. Another is following him, still farther to the north. I'd prefer to land first, without any delay caused by aircraft in front of us.

"Bellingham Tower, Arrow Four-One-Niner-Niner-Seven is ten southwest with Information Tango," I announce on tower frequency.

"Arrow Four-One-Niner-Niner-Seven, Bellingham Tower. Report left base over the river delta for Runway Three-Four. Plan to follow a Bonanza that's about to enter a left downwind."

"Roger, Tower. We have some damage to our tail section after a bird strike during climb-out from Friday Harbor. Negative emergency. The flight controls seem to be fine. But we'd prefer to get on the ground as soon as possible."

The control tower acts immediately to our request, instructing the arriving Bonanza to circle to the west until we're down. Without any hesitation on the part of the controller, he then instructs the Cessna following the Bonanza to reduce speed to let us land first.

"Arrow Niner-Niner-Seven, you're now number one for Runway Three-Four, modified left base at your discretion. Cleared to land."

Our tax dollars at work!

The pitch control system of a Piper Arrow is a bit unique, since it incorporates a stabilator and an anti-servo tab, rather than a traditional horizontal stabilizer and elevator. The entire horizontal surface pivots to provide pitch control. And the leading edge of the stabilator has received the impact.

Our landing at Bellingham is normal, although I concentrate on the flare to make sure there's no unusual binding in the stabilator. We're down and taxing to parking without further incident.

But it was a very big bird.

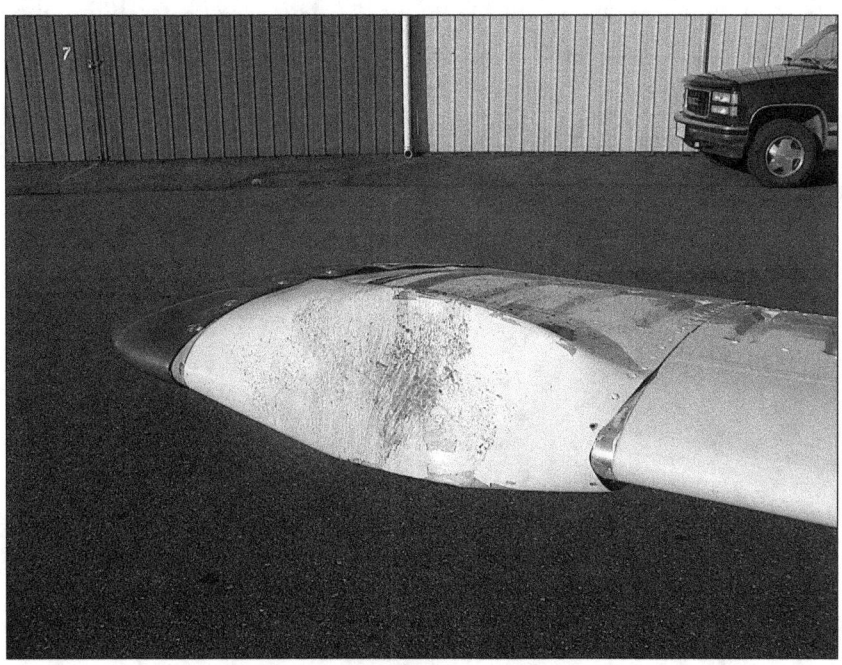

Stabilator damage - bird strike

Parked in front of the hangar, I walk around the tail, checking closely for any additional damage. Fortunately, the whack has been confined to the outer section of the stabilator. It didn't migrate back to the flight-critical anti-servo tab, and damage seems limited to the outer panel of the leading edge. Even the fiberglass wingtip (stabilator tip) seems untouched except for a few popped rivets. I glance into the tail-cone, inspecting the all-important pitch jackscrew that sits inside, since the entire tail received quite a blow. This was a very serious incident that could have progressed into something much worse.

Which leads me to speculate on the coincidence of this encounter with a seagull. The big bird barely missed the prop, an impact that could have spelled disaster. The propeller could have been damaged (very bad), and a speeding carcass hurled through the cockpit's plexiglas windshield might have been even worse.

Back in Friday Harbor sits the home of famous aviation author Ernest K. Gann, one of my all-time favorite writers. When I write, I try to emulate his free-flowing style. Ernie wrote many aviation classics, most of which touched on the odd relationship between luck and coincidence. One of his best books, *Fate is the Hunter*, highlights his aviation career, and questions whether there really is such a thing as luck. Today, near his home in Friday Harbor, Margy and I unknowingly tested the jaws of fate, found luck, and inaugurated the first chapters for my new book. It's enough to make you wonder about coincidence, and avoid thinking too much about luck.

Chapter 4

First Robin of Spring
Orcas and Lopez Island WA

Just when the Arrow is finally getting back in the air, accompanied by a reasonable plan for utilization for book research, I'm grounded by a bird strike. As is often the case with aircraft, the repairs are delayed for lack of parts. In this case, the corrugated aluminum alloy skin is the stumbling block. Piper reports a 90-day backlog on the metal skin, so the local maintenance shop resorts to hunting down the properly grooved sheet metal elsewhere.

The insurance adjuster is now involved, and I'm pleased when he seems to be treating this incident like a routine claim. I relax substantially when the first email from the adjuster carries the title "N41997 vs. B1RD." Getting financial adjustment may be easy, but first the maintenance shop needs to find the metal.

"We don't want to use old skin," says John, the shop chief. "But corrugated sheets are priced way high at the sources I can find."

No, we don't want old skin. But we do want to get back into the air as soon as possible. I also insist on a detailed inspection of the entire empennage, especially the pitch jackscrew and the stabilator's longitudinal support structure. The whack of the seagull could have been transmitted to other critical components in the tail. The shop chief is equally concerned, although it still looks like we've gotten off easy. But in these austere economic times for general aviation, it's a sad state of affairs to learn that common Piper sheet metal isn't on-hand at the factory. The implication is that the Cherokee series isn't currently rolling off the Piper assembly line, and what little metal they have is limited to other production models.

Summer is coming on fast, and the Arrow sits out-of-commission in the hangar. The best season for flying in the Pacific Northwest is about to escape.

Stabilator repair with pins in rivet holes for alignment

* * * * *

BY THE TIME STABILATOR REPAIRS are complete, it's time for the Arrow's annual inspection. John, the shop chief, finds an unusual case of a frozen throttle cable (probably unraveling in its metal shroud, accounting for the prior incident involving the stiff throttle). Then, as the year draws to a close, there's the onset of the rainy months. Meanwhile, I'm spending much of the cold season across the border in British Columbia. Time at my floating cabin on Powell Lake is precious. Enjoying the winter there detracts even more from my goal of flying and writing about airports of the Pacific Northwest.

Back in Bellingham, N41997 sits comfortably in her hangar, now ready to fly. Although it isn't a heated facility, it's still paradise for an airplane that's spent almost all of her existence parked outside in California or in an open-ended T-hangar on the British Columbia coast. There's considerable difference between "outdoors" here in the Pacific Northwest and outside parking in California, where winter sun is more common than cold rain.

Indoor life is a luxury for the Arrow. The availability of electricity in the hangar provides power for a 60-watt bulb to heat and dehumidify the cockpit, as well as an electrical umbilical attached to an exhaust pipe heating element. For extra measure, the crankcase vent is connected to a tube leading to a container with kitty litter inside, an attempt to absorb bad vapors that lurk inside engines remaining idle for longer than they should.

How much of this attention the engine really needs is controversial, but it's an easy process to hook up these connections. Winter weather can be severe in the Pacific Northwest, but N41997 sits in an enclosed hangar with protective umbilical cords nearly as extensive as a rocket on the launch pad at Cape Kennedy. When I slide open the hangar door, she looks happy and well-loved.

But still there's the problem of inactivity. An active airplane is the best medicine for both engine and airframe (to say nothing of avionics). It's important to get back in the air.

* * * * *

IN JANUARY, I FLY FOR THE FIRST TIME since the bird strike. First, I take the Arrow around the pattern for three landings to regain my legal currency. It's a simple step, but I find myself busy in the cockpit, running the climb checklist after takeoff: landing gear, flaps, throttle, prop rpm, mixture control, fuel pump, lights. By the time I'm turning downwind, its time for the landing checklist. Up and down and around the pattern – plenty to do for a pilot as noncurrent as I've become.

But it really is like riding a bicycle, so it all comes back quickly. Quickly, that is, if I get busy with flying. Excuses be gone!

* * * * *

"ARROW FOUR-ONE-NINER-NINER-SEVEN, taxi to Runway Three-Four via Foxtrot, Alpha, and Golf."

It sounds complicated, but I'm becoming used to Bellingham Airport. Foxtrot angles towards the parallel taxiway, Alpha. At the end of Alpha is the run-up area at Golf.

A P-3 Orion and an S-3, both Naval aircraft, have just taken off in sequence on Runway 34. This airport hosts a variety of activity, including MD-80-series airliners, warbirds from the local air museum, amphibians, and occasional operational military aircraft. It's quite a mix that manifests peaks and valleys ranging from very busy to strangely quiet.

Margy makes the takeoff today, while I carefully monitor the engine gauges. She makes a left downwind departure, climbing to 2500 feet. In front of us, the flat fields near the shoreline reflect as a bright white sheen, a result of the previous night's extensive dose of ice-depositing fog. Besides the whitened fields, morning sunlight reflects brilliantly off farmland puddles that have brought this area to flood stage. It's a common condition here during the winter. Yet, most years, the farmers escape serious damage by a very narrow margin. Again this January, the situation looks borderline.

Margy and I fly southbound to Arlington. The morning air is cool and crisp, and the Arrow is performing well.

All is quiet when we arrive at Arlington – unexpected for such a busy little airport on a Saturday morning. We line up as the only traffic, landing to the north. I make the landing, inspecting the runway surface closely on final approach, wondering if the ice-depositing fog could have caked the asphalt with black ice.

Arlington Airport, Washington

As we drop lower, it seems evident the runway is dry. Flare and touchdown are normal, except for the eerie silence at this usually busy airport.

After landing, we taxi to the self-serve fuel island, an impressive array of pumps. Then we visit the adjacent pilot shop, spending a pleasant morning talking with Jan, the shop's owner and browsing the extensive shelves of used aviation books. Pilots and other locals come in for their morning coffee and donuts, a daily ritual at this friendly establishment. Jan's husband, Rick, who has a Canadian background, joins us for coffee. With his extensive experience in flight instruction and aircraft maintenance, we hit it off well, with a lively discussion of books, flying, and the people who make aviation so unique. It reminds me of all that's special about small airports throughout the nation.

Arlington's self-serve fuel island

As more donut and coffee patrons join us, it's standing room only. When we say goodbye and walk outside, the atmosphere has changed. Arlington has morphed into a beehive of activity, with several aircraft taxiing, taking off, and arriving.

The day before, the Arrow's recent inactivity required a battery recharge (again). Now, as Margy rotates the key, the prop barely moves, but she catches the start cycle perfectly. During the short flight to

Arlington, the alternator had little time to help the battery settle back into a normal charging cycle. So rather than risk another engine start today, we head directly back to Bellingham. It's not much of a flight in terms of time, but at least we're getting back into the flying routine.

We follow-up two weeks later with another flight south to test some recent autopilot repairs. George (our autopilot) drives us over the same farmlands we previously traversed on our trip to Arlington, now relatively dry after an extensive period of winter sun, a rare respite in this part of the nation. We circle over Skagit Regional Airport, looking and listening on the radio to determine the level of activity. This is often a busy place, and some of the traffic is typically no-radio.

Burlington-Skagit Regional Airport, Washington

I use George's assistance to lower the Arrow into the traffic pattern, using a 45-degree entry to the downwind to assure I fit into the normal flow. There are several other aircraft in the pattern, as judged by what we see and hear on the radio. Meanwhile, Margy and I keep a watchful eye for no-radio aircraft. I disengage George (who has passed his test flawlessly), and lower the landing gear.

After a full-stop landing, I taxi back to the active runway and depart Skagit as quickly as possible. In the past, I've found this airport to be a high-stress environment, but certainly it's partly because I've become so noncurrent in the Arrow. When things aren't automatic in the cockpit, traffic volume makes a huge difference in your comfort level.

On later flights to Skagit Regional, we'll make a visit to the newly reopened cafe near the Corporate Jet Center. Eating on the patio, where you can watch airplanes come and go, is one of my favorite things, and this small restaurant is just the place to do it.

Today, after our taxi-back on the parallel taxiway, we depart quickly, climbing straight out, then slightly to the right for the return to Bellingham. It isn't much flying, but every little bit helps on the road to getting comfortable again. The weather is beginning to move in, so I knew today's flying would be limited. Already, the mid-level clouds to the south are thickening.

"Had enough?" I ask Margy. "Or would you like to head over to Orcas?"

Fortunately, Margy hasn't had enough. Like me, she's been watching the sky to the south. We both know our limits these days, but there's still plenty of room today for some local flying. We shouldn't go far, and we'll need to keep an eye on the weather, but Orcas Island is only a short hop away. We've discussed scouting out the airport for a camping facility that's supposedly right on the field. In another few months, it will be warm enough to pack our camping gear aboard the Arrow again, and we look forward to it. So I level off at 2000 feet, and we start across the water to the San Juan Islands.

Orcas is in the northern region of the San Juans. I scoot along the north shore of the island, westbound, with Mount Constitution towering to our left. The Garmin 430 GPS gives a beep, the "Terrain Warning" light flashes, and the receiver automatically switches into terrain-avoidance mode.

"Pretty obvious why it did that," I say, glancing over at Margy.

She nods, knowing it's just a case of good equipment telling us what it should. We're well clear of the terrain, but close enough for the GPS to wonder if we've noticed the threatening mountain to our left.

At our 2000-foot altitude, even though we're over the ocean, the towering terrain blocks the view towards Orcas Airport, right around the corner to the left. Even the AWOS automated weather frequency cuts in and out, as we try to determine the surface winds. By the time the AWOS settles into a smooth announcement verifying wind from the north, the airport is poking out from the edge of the ridge, only two miles ahead.

"Orcas Eastsound Traffic, Arrow Four-One-Niner-Niner-Seven is two northwest, planning right traffic for Runway Three-Four."

I'm finally ahead of the airplane for the first time today. I've reviewed the airport diagram on the short flight from Skagit Regional, and I know a landing to the north requires right-hand traffic. What I see when I clear the ridge is exactly what I expect – although considerably more beautiful.

Orcas Eastsound Airport, Washington

I've landed here before, but it's been nearly two decades. The airport has barely changed, but my perception beauty has changed over the years. This is a wonderful little airport on a quaint island. I touch down on Runway 34, forcing myself to concentrate on the approach and block out the beauty for now, which is hard to do, and I make a good landing.

We inspect the grass parking area on our way to the paved ramp, since this is where the airport camping is located. It will be a wonderful spot to spend the night as soon as the weather warms up and the nights get shorter.

From the airport, Margy and I walk the well-marked trail to town. It's a leisurely one-mile hike to Eastsound, where we eat lunch, keeping an eye on the weather that has now ushered in noticeably cooler air and a touch of wind. Still, the clouds remain high and the visibility is superb. It's a fine day for airport hopping, and exactly what the doctor (or flight instructor) ordered for "getting back onto the bicycle."

* * * * *

AT THE END OF FEBRUARY, Margy returns to Powell River to spend some time at our floating cabin, while I remain in Bellingham. One sunny morning, I decide it's the perfect day for a solo flight. Flying alone is a rarity for me, since Margy is usually there to assist me with checklists, even on flights where I'm the sole manipulator of the controls. It's a great luxury to have such assistance, and an outstanding safety backup that I appreciate. So flying solo is a relatively unique experience for me, and makes me appreciate Margy's teamwork in the cockpit even more. It's pretty awkward to cycle through the cylinder head and exhaust gas temperatures on each of the four cylinders in the midst of a solo takeoff run. With Margy along to make the takeoff, I routinely experience such an extravagance.

I've been planning to visit Lopez Island, although my airport directory reminds pilots it's a long walk to town. On a sunny and relatively warm February day, there's no time better than the present.

Lopez is a place I visited, ever so briefly, nearly twenty years ago. But today it will be more than a landing and taxi-back for another takeoff, since I look forward to exploring the island. It's the perfect day for a hike – long-sleeve conditions but no jacket necessary. The sun shines in a nearly cloudless sky, and there's plenty of daylight for the three-mile trek to town and back. I expect the downhill hike will be enough, but I should be able to find a taxicab for the return route. It's the kind of island where an outstretched thumb will probably result in a ride, so I may start walking back on my own without a cab.

There's no traffic in the pattern at Lopez Island. When I departed Bellingham, the wind was light from the north, but I now hear an aircraft report turning downwind for Runway 16 at nearby Friday Harbor. So I decide to land to the south at Lopez, circling around and lining up for a crosswind entry and right traffic. I make a nice landing, with no one to witness it.

Lopez Airport, San Juan Islands

The ramp is empty, except for one other aircraft. This airplane is parked with only a chock and no tie-down ropes, probably another day visitor like me. I turn in close to the fence and swing wide through the marked parking location. When I get out of the Arrow and try to push it back, I encounter a bit of uphill slope. I evaluate the wide clearances in this parking area, and decide to stop pushing and chock the nose-wheel a few feet forward of the official spot. Just to be more comfortable during my absence, I secure the Arrow with a long tie-down rope that barely reaches the metal ring under my left wing.

My hike along Airport Road winds past the golf course that adjoins the airport. A sign on the airport gate reads: "Don't Enter Airport Looking for Golf Balls." Golfers and airplanes can be a miserable match.

I pass roads with names like Wild Duck Lane, finally arriving at Fisherman Bay Road that will take me north to the village. I hike past a large farm, where two Canada Geese are walkin' and honkin' in the field. They pace back and forth in every direction. I wonder if they cleared Customs coming in from Canada. (Oh, this is winter converging on spring, so they're headed north, not south. Canadian Customs will be their next stop.) Finally, they take off to the north, honkin' away and cruising low over the flat fields.

I walk on the right side of the road. There's no paved shoulder, so I consider walking on the other side so I can face traffic. Before I cross over, I notice the body of a large robin right on the edge of the pavement. I step over the bird, but come to a stop in just a few feet.

What could have killed this healthy-looking robin? I can't leave it on the edge of the road. It seems odd to find a full-grown robin here late in February. It would be more logical to find a bird like this, alive or dead, during the heart of spring. Birds die natural deaths all the time, but how often do you find one lying dead in plain sight?

I turn around and look down at this beautiful robin that has ended its life so tragically. Maybe a car hit it, but that seems unlikely. Its body looks undamaged, and its death seems recent, judging by the colorful condition of its feathers.

It seems appropriate to move the robin farther off the road, out of the way of passing motorists. But I don't want to handle a dead animal in a place where I'm unable to wash my hands. So I carefully push it a few feet off the shoulder with my foot, until it rests in a shallow ditch. I toss some grass over its body, and resume my hike down the road, now crossing to the other side.

I stop again. It still doesn't seem right. This bird deserves more. After all, it's a robin, the spirit of the spring season. The ditch in which the robin now rests is where someone (or another animal) may walk. I should move the bird farther from the road. But it's a ways back now, so I resolve to stop here on my way back to the airport and give the bird an appropriate burial.

Soon the road starts noticeably downhill. The airport sits at a field elevation of 200 feet, and the village is at the harbor's sea level, so the math says it will be more of a struggle hiking back up to the airport. The road is wider here, with a large shoulder that makes me more comfortable as I walk. I wind my way down to Fisherman Bay in the sun, on a glorious February day.

Fisherman Bay is masked in the quiet of winter, its primary marina holding only three boats. On a typical summer day, I wouldn't be surprised to find fifty boats here.

Fisherman Bay

At the village, I walk around for a few minutes, looking in the windows of some of the shops. Many are closed this time of year, and the level of activity suits me fine. I'm sure this would be a beautiful place during the summer, but not nearly as peaceful.

I start back to the airport without calling a taxi. The weather remains perfect for hiking, and I need the exercise. Besides, if I take a cab, I'll break my promise of stopping to bury the robin at the side of the road. (On a later visit, Margy and I do try contacting a cab, but learn there are none on the island.)

I stop for a snack at the cafe opposite the marina, and then start up the first major hill, which causes me to question my decision not to take a taxi. I huff and puff, and even sweat a bit in the cool air. A man on a bicycle passes me, also climbing uphill, barely moving in low gear. I watch him disappear out of site over the crest of the road. The grade now begins to level off, and the worst is behind.

When I approach the area where I've left the robin, I look down and walk slower, making sure I don't overshoot the spot. It would be hard to miss, since the colorful bird is large and vibrant looking, even after his life has ended. I stop and look down thoughtfully at its graceful, strong body.

"You deserve a nice burial," I say out loud. "You're a beautiful bird, just like you've always been. And robins like you make people awfully happy. Hopeful too."

I reach down, using my bare hands to move the fine bird farther from the road. I find a spot near the barbed wire fence surrounding the farm, and place the bird in a dry place, with his head and distinctly robust beak pointed to the side.

"There. Now you can rest here and watch the world go by. You're part of the earth, as we all are. We're all tied together on this world, you know. And we always will be. Thanks for bringing happiness to this island."

It's a little childish, but I don't hesitate. There are plenty of loose twigs lying nearby, so I gather them and lay them over the robin's body in a mound: "There, that will keep you warm."

I step back onto the road and hike the short distance up to Airport Road. By the time I turn the corner, I'm humming to myself, pleased to be alive and hiking along this island road on a peaceful winter day. Here in late February, a bird symbolizing the approaching spring has brought me, simultaneously, sadness and joy. It's a strange combination, but one that I somehow accept.

Chapter 5

Flying with Fred

Southern California and Coastal British Columbia

FRED FLINTSTONE, JUNIOR, is the mascot of the Mount San Antonio College Flying Team, a group of students who compete throughout the United States in collegiate level competitive flight events. Some would call him merely a stuffed child's toy, but he's more than that to these college students. Born in the back room of an arcade in southern California, a location frequented by the Mt SAC Flying Team, Fred has seen his share of the aviation world.

During an evening of shoot-'em-up video battles and token-operated skillball, team members gathered thousands of points in paper redemption tickets. Kristina, who was elected to handle the financial role, proudly collected these brown coupons. She hauled around enough tickets to make you think the flying team was about to cash in for a Porsche. In reality, they were wavering between a huge hand-launched model airplane (the team already possessed three) and a large stuffed mascot. Thus, on this momentous evening, Fred was adopted.

The prize – sorry, Fred, I know you're really a person – was claimed by Adam, radio call sign "Grunt," the proud captain of the top ranked community college flying team in the United States. That night, Fred quietly rode home with his new dad, destined to become a man of the modern world.

Between flight competitions, Fred wanted to contribute more to the team's daily activities. So Adam created a new role for him. Instructors at the college's flight school approach their jobs, as is typical of the trade, with a relatively professional yet fun-loving demeanor.

Their training flights are laced with endless hours of placid challenge, punctuated by moments of sheer terror. Student pilots have a way of suddenly getting a flight instructor's attention at the most awkward moments, such as during short final on a gusty day. Fred was often along for the ride.

Fred's job was to fly with the instructors and their students on "exotic trips" in Cessna 150s and 152s. He served as an excellent passenger, never critical of the piloting skills he witnessed (at least in public). But two-seat Cessnas have no back seat. So with the student and instructor in the front, Fred was subjugated to riding in the small baggage compartment. Fortunately, in these aircraft, the baggage compartment has it's own windows, for reasons known only to Cessna Aircraft Company.

The college's flying team presented Fred with his own pilot's logbook, and each flight instructor was required to complete the entries for each flight with exactness. Fred soon logged over a hundred hours during flights to exciting destinations with names like Blythe, Needles, Bakersfield, Corona, Barstow, and Apple Valley (now there's a misnomer) – mostly hot desert locales where no sensible person travels during the summer. There's nothing like bouncing around in a baggage compartment during summer trips across the desert at terrain-hugging heights, high enough to clear the ridges, but low enough to extract all of the turbulence from the tumbling air mass. Fred also landed at larger airports, including Santa Barbara and Palm Springs, so he considered himself a member of the jet set.

Everyone at the flight school adored Fred, and he helped the flying team win two national championships in a row. As the team's faculty advisor, I asked Adam if Fred could go on a lengthy trip to Canada with me. Of course, everyone would miss Fred, but it would give him the opportunity to see another country. And think of the flying hours he would be able to log.

"Imagine!" said Fred. "I'll be exploring another country in a roomy four-seat airplane on an international flight!"

Fred promised to write home regularly, keeping dad and his many friends updated on his adventures.

This is Fred's story, as only he could tell it.

* * * * *

I, FRED FLINTSTONE, JUNIOR, of Mt SAC Flying Team fame, was thrilled about this project from the very beginning. When Adam told me I was going on a "real" cross-country flight, a journey to Canada, I was proud to have the opportunity to carry the American flag to foreign soil. My logbook would hold evidence of my celebrity status as a visitor to destinations such as Toronto, Ottawa, and Montreal, or so I thought. Wayne explained there are other places even more beautiful than those prestigious cities.

I'll learn to ride in boats, ATVs, and kayaks, and fly to places few others have ever visited. I hope they have hot showers and flush toilets.

The days before my departure for Canada are filled with incidents that make me wonder what I'm getting into. Since I tend to believe everything anyone tells me, I'm easily fooled. Wayne takes advantage of this, and begins to play a frustrating game with me. I'm loaded aboard a Piper Arrow, where I get my own seat behind the pilots and occasionally up front as pilot-in-command! But it appears there are a few side-trips scheduled first, so I go along for the ride.

Fred Flintstone, Jr., pilot in command

* * * * *

THE ANNOYING GAME Wayne plays with me involves visiting locations completely unlike Canada, where he tries to fool me into believing we've arrived in British Columbia. Of course, I'm never really fooled, but I'm a bit embarrassed by the challenge. I keep trying to figure out whether Wayne is kidding or not. It's hard to tell. Few people understand his distorted sense of humor.

My first photo with N41997 shows me propped up on the Arrow's cowling at San Diego International Airport. At first I think this is Vancouver because Wayne asks me how I like Canada. But to me, it's just like the good ol' USA – airplanes everywhere. None of the air traffic controllers are talking Canadian, so I'm quite sure this is Wayne's idea of a joke.

San Diego International Airport

* * * * *

ONE EVENING, WHILE I'M STILL TRYING to figure out this game, we land at Desert Center, a remote airport in the high desert of southern California. This is one of Wayne's favorite observing spots as an amateur astronomer. During the summer, you need to land near sunset. Any earlier and the temperature exceeds 100. Oh, that's Fahrenheit, since I haven't learned the Canadian Celsius thermometer scale yet. An arrival after dark is even worse, since there aren't any runway lights. So it takes some precise scheduling for a summer visit to Desert Center.

Meade LX-90 Schmidt-Cassegrain telescope at Desert Center

This interesting location possesses some possibilities, since it meets the criteria Wayne has used to describe Canada – remote, sparkling skies, quiet. But the sand and heat don't seem quite right. Remote is one thing – bleak is quite another.

After a very dark night (and a nice view of the Ring Nebula), we pack up our tent before sunrise, attempting to beat the heat. I enjoy my visit, but this certainly isn't the British Columbia rainforest.

Camping at Desert Center Airport, California

* * * * *

I FINALLY ARRIVE IN CANADA, where I find myself sitting on the wing of the Piper Arrow at an airport named Nanaimo, clasping my passport proudly. Judging by the length of today's flight, this has got to be Canada. Actually, I don't have a passport, but Wayne has placed me here with his passport to greet two women in Canadian Customs uniforms, now approaching the aircraft. I hope they have a sense of humor.

CanPass has simplified entry into Canada for private aircraft, but today I'm expecting complications. We're carrying book-publishing products we'll need to declare, and Wayne seems a bit nervous about the process. He telephoned the Nanaimo Customs office from Oregon to explain we're carrying promotional materials and the necessary paperwork (the dreaded Canadian B-3 form). Customs agents don't get to harass private aircraft very often. Something tells me this is the day.

Wayne greets the two young officers in a jovial manner they're probably not accustomed to: "This is Fred. I forgot to declare him when I telephoned," says Wayne. "But, as you can see, he has a passport, and he'll be traveling with us in Canada."

Clearing Customs at Nanaimo, British Columbia

The older woman (probably in her thirties) throws a faint smile at me. Or is it a scowl? Does she wonder if I really have my own passport?

Walking beside the agent-in-charge is a woman who looks younger and equally stern. There's a look of confusion on her face. Maybe I spoiled her planned greeting of "Welcome to Canada," and she's wondering whether it's still appropriate.

"Oh, my," says the young woman.

That's it – just a muted "Oh, my." It seems to go downhill from there.

It doesn't take long to discern these Customs agents are going to be thorough. I hope it wasn't something I didn't say.

Wayne, in his typical over-reaction mode seems primed for trouble. It becomes Margy's job to calm the situation, which isn't an easy task. The senior agent demands that every item in our airplane be removed. They inspect each piece of baggage, and open all the bags and containers. Wayne is questioned about a small carrying case containing a vitamin bottle, a computer cable, and a telescope lens.

"Strange place to carry medicine, and why are you bringing a telescope lens into Canada?"

One item at a time, please. You're stressing Wayne to his limit, especially after he's been told to unload a very full airplane on a hot summer day. I happen to know he hates physical labor, and an afternoon sweat isn't a good way to keep his aggravation in check.

"You sure carry a lot of stuff," says the younger woman.

"When you travel in a small airplane, you use every nook and cranny," replies Wayne.

He hasn't completely lost his cool yet, but I can tell it's getting closer, particularly when the Customs agents open the various compartments of the aircraft toolkit. Suspicious tools: a crescent wrench and screwdriver, to say nothing of a sparkplug gapping tool. Fifteen minutes through the ordeal, Wayne unwisely turns to his universally misunderstood sense of humor.

"You know, it's going to be a lot of work to load all of these bags back into this tiny airplane. Since I unloaded everything, I assume it's appropriate for you to reload it."

"Oh, no, we aren't allowed to do that," says the senior agent.

On this tarmac today, there's both a communication and generation gap.

Thirty minutes into the hour-long "event," the older agent explains that her assistant is in training and hasn't previously inspected a private aircraft. If this on-the-job training announcement was intended as an explanation to appease Wayne, it was better left unmentioned.

I sit on the wing, watching the proceedings. Wayne's face is getting red, and it isn't from the Canadian sunshine. The young woman reaches into the baggage compartment, picks up a telephone (the old-fashioned kind with a connection cord), and casts a look of suspicion at it.

"Why are you traveling with a telephone? Will you be leaving this in Canada?" she asks.

Visitors must declare all goods they intend to leave in Canada. At the time, all three of us were U.S. citizens, without Canadian permanent residency status. An undeclared telephone would be difficult to explain.

"No, I'll be taking it back to the States with me," replies Wayne. "I carry it in case I need to make a telephone call along the way."

Finally, I see a hint of a smile cross the agent's face.

"Oh, sure, that makes sense," she counters. "Everyone carries a hard-wire phone when they travel, eh?"

Next, the agents gloss over a hundred T-shirts, quickly accepting Wayne's statement that they're for promotional giveaways and are on the declaration list. Instead, they're concerned with a whistle in the aircraft survival kit, and then they closely inspect a flashlight and its spare batteries (sealed in their original container). They ask about a full-size electric fan, but Wayne has a perfectly stupid (and acceptable) answer.

"No air conditioning at our cabin. I always travel with a fan."

Oh, sure, the fan is going back to the States, too. These agents aren't looking for minor violations – they're looking for newsworthy items. Sure enough, with all of the suspicious camping gear out of the rear baggage compartment, the senior agent is now instructing the younger woman regarding the hollow area behind the aft bulkhead. In our case, the only items to inspect in this crawl-space are control cables and remotely mounted aircraft radios.

As the inspection draws to a close, Wayne refuses to speak to the agents unless they ask their questions twice. As he becomes increasingly indignant, I get worried, knowing this is risking a mark on my future immigration record. But Wayne seems willing to continue with his silly game of "Say again," to make sure the agents know he's not a satisfied customer.

The continued reddening of Wayne's face serves as an ugly indicator of disturbed international tensions. As a new visitor to Canada, I'm beginning to wonder about this trip to such a highly militarized land.

Finally, the agent-in-charge announces the inspection is complete. Margy insists on going to the office to fine-tune the import fee calculations, while Wayne reloads the airplane. (Meanwhile, I sit and supervise.) It's obvious Margy is trying to keep Wayne out of the office, and wisely so.

Margy returns to report the fees we computed on our forms were accepted as correct and paid. She also notes the agents started to warm a bit when they began to understand that our declared imports are for a book about Canada. Wayne always carries copies of his books in his backpack, and he often gives them away to anybody (else) that mutters a positive word about his publishing projects. Not today.

Afterwards, I reflect on the obvious – it's fortunate my first visit to this foreign country didn't result in immigration prison.

* * * * *

A FEW MINUTES LATER, we're taxiing across the Nanaimo ramp to the fuel pumps at the nearby fixed-base operator. As we exit the airplane, the gas attendant greets us, while his friends sit on the office porch nearby.

"We watched all the unloading and reloading you went through on the hot tarmac in the Customs box," says the jovial fellow. "So we decided you deserve the bulk fuel price discount today."

"In that case, fill 'er up," says Wayne with a laugh.

It turns out this is our lucky day, after all.

* * * * *

THE FLIGHT FROM NANAIMO to Powell River is a short one, but Wayne has enough time to calm down. Apparently the hardest part of the journey is over for him. When we finally land in Powell River, he's looking a lot less red-faced. The climate here obviously agrees with him.

It takes almost an hour to remove everything from the airplane (again), load the car, and secure the aircraft. I supportively cheer on these efforts from my rather unceremonious position in the back seat of a 1989 Ford Tempo. My head is shoved facing rearward in the seat (temporary, I'm sure).

When the work is finished, I'm removed from the car, propped up on the nose cowling of the Arrow and pose for my arrival photo. British Columbia, I'm finally here!

Fred arrives at Powell River, BC

* * * * *

PROBABLY THE BEST WAY to tell the story of my travels in Canada is to share a few of the email messages I sent home to my dad, Adam, in California. In a nutshell, this trip wasn't all I expected, but I wouldn't have traded the experience for a trip to Ottawa, or even Montreal.

* * * * *

July 9
Dear Adam,
   This Canada thing has turned out to be a lot different than I expected. Right now I'm sitting in the front seat of an old Ford Tempo at a marina, awaiting the return of Wayne and Margy from their float cabin. They promise to take me there soon, but their boat was so full of junk when they departed the dock yesterday there was no room for me. But that's okay, since it has hardly stopped raining since

I arrived, and you know how much I hate to get my hairdo wet. At least from the front seat of the car, I can watch all of the boats coming and going all day long.

Now, I'm not one to complain, but Wayne talks continually about boats these days, so I was really looking forward to my first ride. Finally, I got to drive my first boat, but it was a lot different than I thought it would be. It wasn't nearly as exciting as departure stalls in a 152.

Did you hear the latest? – Wayne plans to write a chapter in one of his books about my adventures. He says people who want to learn about unusual things will read my story. I'm sure he's talking about Canada and not me. As for book material, it's true that I'm quite photogenic.

I hope to send pictures soon from places with weird Canadian names.
Love,
Fred

On the command bridge

* * * * *

July 14
Dear Adam,

I went kayaking today. After the big buildup, it was a bit of a disappointment. But my hairdo survived the ordeal. I was a big hit with the babes on the beach.

As you probably know, the guy in the rear seat of a kayak does all of the navigation (rudder pedals in back, if you can imagine that). I quickly learned I could stop paddling and make the babe in front do all of the work. She never even knows when you're goofing off. Don't I look simply dashing as captain of the ship?

Personally, I prefer playing pool at the video arcade in California. Of course, that's where I was born.

It has stopped raining for now. The temperature got up to nearly 80 today (on our American Fahrenheit scale). Say hello to all of my buddies on the flying team. When I get home, I'll have lots of stories to tell.

Love,
Fred

Captain of the Kayak

* * * * *

July 17
Dear Adam,

When we travel in the car, things get pretty tight, so I volunteer to ride on top in the kayak. The girls at the gas station waved to me today and wanted to know what my name is. Apparently, they don't know many guys named Fred in this country.

Wayne brags about me to everyone we meet. He loves to tell the story about how I fly in airplanes and have my own logbook.

I'm having fun in this country. I'm not exactly sure what it means, but everyone says 'Eh' all the time.

See you in 22 days (but who's counting).
Love,
Fred

* * * * *

July 20
Dear Adam,
All of this boat stuff is fine, but I was born to fly. After all, that's why you adopted me.

Finally, I got to do some flying. We went to a place called Bella Bella. No, I'm not stuttering. Of course, when we arrived, we looked at boats in the harbor. To be truthful, Adam, I'm getting just a bit sick of all of these boats. But we got in some good flying, too.

We camped beside the airplane, although one of the locals told stories about recent bear and cougar sightings. During an evening walk to the end of the runway, Wayne found bear tracks. I hardly slept at all that night. In the morning we were awakened by two Grumman Geese taking off, followed by a Beaver on floats. Lots of animals here.
Love,
Fred

Camping at Bella Bella Airport, BC

* * * * *

July 24
Dear Adam,
I hate to brag, but this Canada thing is starting to work out, now that I'm adjusted. Wayne kept telling me we have to be careful because of bears and mountain lions, so I was pretty scared at first. But today I met my first mountain

SeaFair at Powell River, BC

lion. He was huge, but not a problem at all. In fact, he asked if he could have his picture taken with me. I guess he had never seen a handsome guy like me riding in a kayak on top of a car.

Oh, I shouldn't tell you this, because I don't want you to worry, but I think Wayne completely forgot about me the other day. We were at a marina, and Wayne got to talking to this guy at the dock about boats and airplanes. Then everybody walked away, and I assumed it would be just for a minute. When Wayne came back a few hours later he was real apologetic.

I'll be home in 16 days (but who's counting?). Of course, that's only if Wayne doesn't leave me in Oregon by mistake.

Love,
Fred

* * * * *

August 8
Dear Adam,

I've been sitting in the back seat of the car for days, waiting for something to happen. Finally, Wayne showed up to announce we're goin' home. Whoopee!

I don't understand why Wayne and Margy are so grumpy about going home. They think they're Canadians. As for me, I'm a Los Angeles homeboy, and I'm ready to leave. Of course, nothing seems to be on schedule on this airline. Flights just begin when Wayne and Margy are ready to go, and that could be almost anytime.

Love,
Fred

* * * * *

August 9
Dear Adam,

On the way home, we stopped on the Oregon coast to camp. What I didn't know about Oregon is the beaches are cold and cloudy most of the time. We dropped under the overcast and bounced down onto a tiny runway by the ocean. Margy really plopped it in this time, and Wayne yelled something obscene, for which he apologized to me later.

As it was getting dark, Wayne hustled me out of the airplane to get a photo. "Hurry up Fred, it's cold," he said. So he took a quick picture, and then I was tossed back into the plane to spend the night while everyone else got to sleep in a cozy tent.

My traveling adventures in Canada are now over, and I saw a lot. Everybody liked me, although the U.S. Customs inspector yesterday asked if I was a kid's toy. That really annoyed me (Wayne too). But now I'm finally on my way home. Here comes the sun!

Love,
Fred

Camping at Siletz Bay Airport, GlenEden Beach, Oregon

◊ ◊ ◊ ◊ ◊ ◊ ◊

Chapter 6

International Incident
Powell River BC

DURING MY MANY FLIGHTS TO CANADA as a U.S. tourist, border crossing was nearly flawless. The unload-the-airplane confrontation with Fred at Nanaimo (Chapter 5) was the only exception, and even that run-in with Customs faded over time.

So simple was the border crossing procedure that it became notably relaxed. (After September 11, 2001, of course, it was never the same.) As a CanPass member, a simple phone call to Canadian authorities would set the stage for an efficient entry. One memorable check-in by phone reminds me of the low-key approach for CanPass arrivals. My toll-free phone call from Astoria was answered (in Ottawa?) with a simple "Hello," which made me wonder if I'd dialed the wrong number.

"Is this CanPass?" I asked.

"Good morning. Do you have a border crossing request?"

"Yes, this is a U.S. citizen in a private aircraft at Astoria, Oregon, and I'd like to enter Canada at Campbell River, British Columbia, at 1915 Zulu, 2:15 pm local time."

"What's your aircraft identification number," asked the youthful-sounding man.

"November Four-One-Nine-Nine-Seven," I replied.

A brief pause, while I heard the clicking of a keyboard on the other end of the line.

"Is this Wayne?" asked the friendly voice.

"Yes, it is," I replied with a bit of shock at the informality.

"Is Margaret with you today?"

"Yes, she is."

It doesn't get any better than this. When you carry a clean record, the efficiency of the computer age has its benefits. Welcome to Canada.

* * * * *

IN 2008, MY DAYS as an American tourist ended. After waiting two years for our application to be approved, Margy and I became permanent residents of Canada. It's the equivalent of Canadian citizenship without voting rights.

No longer would we need to limit our stay to 180 days per year. Now Margy and I could come and go as we pleased. But not so when flying an airplane. In fact, our border-crossing situation with N41997 changed dramatically for the worse. The N-prefix was the source of the problem.

Regulations allow Canadian citizens and permanent residents to enter the country in a private vehicle (car, boat, or airplane), but only if the vehicle is registered in Canada. Whereas previously N41997 was welcome in Canada with a U.S. pilot at the controls, she was now banned from entry when piloted by a Canadian resident. One way around this limitation would be to simply (or not so simply, depending on who you asked) register the airplane in Canada. In our case, it was far from simple.

We evaluated the alternatives. Even though we were willing to pay the costly taxes Canada would grab from registration of the airplane, that wasn't the end to the complications. The N-number would have to be repainted as a C-identifier (a minor factor), and resale of the airplane in the U.S. in a future decade would necessitate re-registration in the States (getting more complicated). But the real difficulty centered on the licensing of the pilots, including both my commercial and flight instructor certificates (plus instrument rating) and Margy's private pilot certificate. Plus, new Canadian medical certificates would be required for both of us. Since I operate in the U.S. on an annual special issuance of my medical certificate due to my cardiovascular history, the last thing I wanted was to be examined under new Canadian medical standards. Who knows what would happen if I had to start all over again?

In summary, my desire was to resolve the issue by finding a legal way to enter Canada in N41997 without a change in national registration. Since I had flown across the border freely as a U.S. tourist, it would seem there should be a way to continue such operations now that I'm officially a Canadian resident.

That's when I decided to hire a Canadian aviation lawyer to resolve my situation. It seemed like a good idea at the time, even although I knew significant legal fees would be involved. What I didn't know was the conclusions of the lawyer (after lots of wasted motion) wouldn't provide me with any real guidance nor a realistic new direction to pursue. But I was right about one thing – the legal fees were astronomical.

With this avenue a dead end, I began to investigate aircraft rental during my stay in Canada. Such a solution is somewhat less complex, but it didn't resolve my real thirst for flying in Canada. Among other limitations is the lack of rental aircraft at Powell River. Westview Flying Club's Cessna 172 is a fine deal for renters, but getting used to a lower-performance airplane without sophisticated avionics is a lot like learning how to live with a boat that's a trawler after being used to a planing cruiser.

So, in the end, the decision was simple – keep the Arrow hangared in Bellingham, and fly her during my trips to the States. N41997 would never again cruise the skies of Canada, a sad outcome, but it would rest comfortably (especially during the wet winter) in an enclosed hangar, ready for U.S. adventures every time I return to Bellingham.

In a way, this forced me to explore the skies of Washington and Oregon. All recreational pilots need reasons (or at least excuses) to fly. Although I had landed at many of the region's coastal airports during my trips to and from Canada, now I could concentrate in exploring in more detail the destinations of the Pacific Northwest.

Chapter 7

Why Are We Going to Seattle?
Bremerton and Ocean Shores WA

"Niner-Niner-Seven, be advised I'm getting a double hit on your transponder," reports Victoria Terminal.

I pause for a moment, and glance at Margy in the left seat. She shakes her head as if she doesn't understand either. So I reply like I often do when I need some time to think.

"Niner-Niner-Seven. Roger."

In other words, thanks for whatever you're telling me.

"Must be just a false target," I say to Margy over the intercom. "But keep a close eye for traffic."

We're climbing out of Bellingham, IFR southbound, intercepting our assigned radial from Whatcom VOR. The weather is superb, especially for early-March – severe clear and unseasonably warm. A huge high-pressure system sits overhead, which should protect the Pacific Northwest for at least two more days. The IFR route south involves a quick handoff to Victoria while we pass through a sliver of their airspace covering the area just south of Bellingham. In a few minutes, we'll be back with U.S. controllers at Whidbey Island.

"Conflict alert," reports the Victoria controller. "Traffic at eleven o'clock, less than a mile, northbound. Type unknown. Appears to be climbing out of 2000 feet."

We're climbing in the opposite direction, converging with the traffic, but we're already out of 4000 feet. That may explain the "double hit" on our transponder. The controller's scope shows two targets so close together they overlap.

"Niner-Niner-Seven is looking for the traffic," I reply.

Margy and I watch with concentration for the next few miles, never seeing anything, which isn't uncommon in situations like this. Then the radio report is what we're waiting for.

"Niner-Niner-Seven, clear of previously issued traffic."

"Thanks, Victoria. Niner-Niner-Seven."

As expected, Victoria hands us off to Whidbey Approach Control. We level at seven thousand, and settle into cruise. George is driving the airplane now, locked on the airway with altitude-hold engaged. I settle back to review the airport directory, while Margy scans for traffic.

"So Bremerton sounds okay to you?" I ask.

As is often the case, we have a destination in mind, but we don't confirm it until we're in the air. Sometimes conditions cause us to change our minds early in the flight, especially once we're high enough to evaluate the actual weather conditions. Meteorological reports and forecasts are fine, but there's nothing like sitting at 7000 feet, being able to look in all directions. It's an amazing perspective on the actual atmospheric conditions.

"Sounds good to me," replies Margy. "The ferry to Seattle should be fun."

Bremerton had never been on our list of destinations, but there's a ferry to Seattle we plan to try for the first time. We've overflown Bremerton so often that I feel familiar with the long runway, but we've never landed. Our plan is to stay overnight at a hotel within walking distance of the ferry terminal, taking the boat to Seattle the next day.

As we approach the Seattle Class B airspace, ATC turns us off the airway well north of Bremerton and provides radar vectors towards downtown Seattle. It's a pretty day, with a great view of the Seattle waterfront. We're getting farther off the direct route to Bremerton.

"Must be part of their local traffic procedures," I suggest over the intercom. "Keeps the airspace open for SeaTac departures to the west."

We're instructed to descend to 3000 feet, still headed directly towards the Space Needle, a nice panorama. By now, SeaTac departures can climb over us safely, so our route makes sense. In a few more minutes, still pointed at the Needle, Seattle Approach Control instructs us to turn towards Bremerton, setting us up for a visual approach.

Traffic in the pattern consists of two other airplanes well ahead of us. I handle the landing, flying a tight pattern, and making a smoother-than-normal landing. Conditions are perfect, with a light wind right down the runway and almost no convection in the relatively cool (warm to us) March air.

Bremerton Airport, Washington

At the self-serve gas facility, we figure out how to pump our gas, although it takes several tries. As important as proper fueling procedures are for small airplanes, I'm always distressed by how different each self-serve station can be. There should be complete standardization to prevent errors. In this case, getting the gas aboard is only part of the challenge. Now how do we pay for it?

There's no credit card reader, and a sign says "Pay Inside." But where? There's a building nearby that looks promising, but the sign over the door says "Flight School." When in doubt, ask Margy to help.

"Would you mind trying to figure out how to pay?"

"Sure. Why don't you taxi to parking while I do it."

She's right. There's a Bonanza behind us, waiting for this side of the pumps.

Bremerton's self-serve fuel

I hop aboard the Arrow and make a quick check of the parking configuration in the "Brown Book" (Airguide's Flight Guide, a popular airport diagram publication). Then I start the engine and taxi to the ramp that's closest to the airport cafe. Restaurants at small airports are usually superb, and it should be a good location to find a taxicab to town.

In this case, the cafe is listed in the Brown Book as a diner, a long building that takes the shape of a classic eatery. There are plenty of open tie-down spaces, so I pick a spot, turn off the engine, and wait for Margy to return from the flight school.

When Margy arrives back at the airplane, we unload our baggage (one small rolling suitcase), and walk to the gate near the diner. A sign near the exit says: "Overnight Tie-down $4.00."

But where? Once again, it isn't clear where you should pay. The parking envelopes are stored here, but there are no instructions where to pay. With no drop-box, the main terminal seems to be where we should go, so that's where we head.

The main door to the terminal is locked. This is a recently constructed palatial building, but no one is home. Like a lot of airports these days, government funding is available for a new terminal, but the poor economy doesn't allow commuter airlines to fill it.

We try a door farther down the side of the building, which is unlocked, but this seems to be mostly empty office space. As we look around the lobby, a young man in a suit steps out of the elevator.

"Hi, do you know where we can pay our overnight parking fee?" asks Margy.

"I haven't a clue," says the blond fellow. "Maybe there's a drop-box somewhere outside."

At this point, I'm perfectly willing to forget the whole thing. How many people would trudge around an airport, dragging their luggage, looking for a place to pay a four-dollar parking bill? Yet, Margy is always concerned with paying what she owes, so we keep looking.

Outside the terminal, there are some mailboxes, so she walks over and tries to find one with an airport office label. There are only numbers on the boxes.

Bremerton parking ramp near diner

"I'll try the flightline side," she says.

"Okay, I'll meet you in the diner."

As I walk towards the restaurant, Margy peels off towards the gate leading back to the parking ramp. Then she walks down the tarmac on the flightline side of the terminal, looking for a drop-box. She finally finds one, but I wonder how often others go to the trouble of following this payment procedure to completion. Sometimes it's impossible to find someone to take your cash.

The diner is fabulous! Good food, great service, and a model aircraft decor, to say nothing of a fine view of real airplanes out the glass wall of windows. Try it – you'll like it.

As is the case with many airport restaurants, you can tell that most of the clientele are locals – airplane buffs but not pilots. When we leave, the car parking lot outside is nearly full. Locals come and go as we wait for our taxi.

The ride to town takes a while. Bremerton Airport is a long way from the small city, but it makes for a scenic drive past the sprawling shipbuilding dry docks. There are plenty of marine jobs here, many of them related to the Navy's fleet maintenance program. We pass destroyers and other big ships, even an aircraft carrier.

"The best jobs in town," says the taxi driver. "Some cutbacks lately, but still a good place to work."

The Hampton Inn is in a scenic location, with a view of the harbor and easy walking distance to the ferry terminal. After checking in, we walk to the Coldstone Creamery nearby. The ice cream tastes great on a relatively warm March evening.

In the twilight, we hike a few hundred more feet, and we're in the spacious ferry terminal. We check tomorrow's schedules for Seattle, and watch one of the ferries coming into dock. There are only a few foot passengers in the terminal, awaiting the arrival of the boat, so we sit with them. When they start to individually leave the waiting area to walk to the departure ramp, we follow them to see how the boarding procedure works.

We stop at the departure gate, while the outgoing passengers continue along the ramp towards the arriving ferry. I look down the tunnel-like structure and see the ferry approaching the dock, brilliant lights blaring straight at us. We stay here long enough to watch the passengers come off the ship, at least fifty of them, day-trippers from Bremerton returning from the big city.

*****

BACK AT THE HOTEL, I tune in the Vancouver Winter Olympics, watching the preliminary bobsled runs and finals for short-track skate racing. As an "almost Canadian," it's fun to see the excitement at Whistler. Both the U.S. and Canada are this year's stars, so it's all good.

The next morning, we take the elevator down to the lobby from our room on the third floor. Our hotel reservation includes one more night, after our boat trip to Seattle. We plan to take advantage of the hotel's free continental breakfast, and then take the next ferry to Seattle. We'll walk around the Seattle waterfront, wander around the tourist shops, and find a place for lunch. But we're really not interested in tourist shops, and what's so great about lunch in Seattle?

The elevator pings and comes to a halt at the second floor. A young couple steps aboard. Apparently they're tourists like us, exploring the area.

"Have you taken the ferry to Seattle?" I ask.

"No, we came in last night in our own boat. Leaving this morning."

So they're just passing through, like us, but they're not including Seattle in their visit. After all, if you own your own boat, you don't need a ferry. Do we?

The elevator pings again, and we're in the lobby. As the young couple steps out, I say to Margy: "Why are we going to Seattle?"

"We don't have to," she replies immediately.

We stand in the elevator looking at each other. The door starts to close, and still we stand there. I push the door-open button, and we're looking out into the lobby again, but neither of us steps out.

"It's a nice day for flying," I say.

"Not many of those in March," she replies.

The door closes again, and the elevator stands motionless with us inside. Margy and I can make decisions quickly without a lot of discussion.

"Let's get outta' here," I say. "We can be airborne right after breakfast."

"Okay with me."

I hit the button for "3rd Floor," and we go back up to our room to pack our small bag.

* * * * *

BEFORE DEPARTING BREMERTON, we made a room reservation at Ocean Shores, an airport I've always wanted to visit. Our departure from Bremerton will involve a turn to the west, and we'll be quickly on our way.

Once airborne, we climb towards the Washington coast, communicating with Seattle Approach and then Seattle Center for VFR flight following and traffic advisories. It's a simple and direct route, ending at Ocean Shores, a cute little airport with a fairly short runway but with unobstructed approaches on both ends. The weather remains cool enough to keep density altitude low for our departure tomorrow, and we're light in fuel and baggage weight, so it's the perfect opportunity for operating a Piper Arrow on a 2700-foot strip.

A few miles east of Ocean Shores, we check the recorded weather on Hoquiam Airport's AWOS. Winds are light from the north, which should favor Runway 33 at Ocean Shores.

I fly the approach, first passing over the runway to check the windsock, verifying that a landing to the north is best. The pattern is right-hand, with a light twin aircraft taxiing out from the parking ramp. I join the right downwind leg.

"Four-Eight-Three is taxiing for Runway 33, with the airplane on downwind in sight," reports the twin on Unicom frequency. "We'll await your landing."

"Okay, thanks." I feel a bit informal about my reply, but it's that kind of place.

I keep my base leg nice and square, but I delay the turn to final, resulting in a sloppy overshoot. As I bank back onto final, I know the twin-engine pilot is watching. I overshoot again, S-turning down final approach.

"I bet you wish you could fly like this," I say on Unicom.

Silence.

"You gotta' learn sometime," I add.

The laugh on frequency tells me this pilot understands. He probably remembers some of his earlier landings.

Ocean Shores Airport, Washington

Exiting the runway, we park on the big apron. At the restroom entrance, I find a key hanging on the wall labeled "Office." So I let myself into the small waiting room, leaving a copy of *Up the Airway*, my first aviation book, on the table. I've had good luck with the honesty of fellow pilots. With an autographed copy labeled "Airport Copy – Do Not Remove," the book is likely to remain in place for years.

The route to the hotel is obvious, since there's only one road leading from the airport. Margy and I walk in single-file along the side of the narrow road, paralleling a ditch. The dirt shoulder is rough and definitely not designed for tourists walking from the airport. The weather for our walk is enjoyable, but the town fathers might look into providing walkways for "tourons" like us, although I doubt many visitors arrive by air.

In an area where the road is clear of cars, I step out onto the pavement where it's smoother for the rollers of the bag I'm pulling. There, that's better.

Road to town from Ocean Shores Airport

A woman in a white SUV pulls up beside us to offer a ride.

"Thanks," I reply. "But we want to get some exercise today."

"Enjoy!" she says.

The SUV does a three-point U-turn in the middle of the road, headed back where she came from. So she must have passed us a few minutes ago, and turned around to offer us a ride. We should have accepted her generosity.

"Thanks, again!" I yell as she completes her turn.

"No problem!" I hear her yell as she stomps on the accelerator and speeds away.

As we approach the town of Ocean Shores, I actually start to sweat (in March). Fortunately, the dirt shoulder has turned to sidewalk on this stretch of the road. We pass an interesting-looking taco stand.

"Looks like our kind of place," I say.

"We can come back later," replies Margy. "Reminds me of Southern California."

It's hard to beat Los Angeles for Mexican restaurants. And we're still getting used to Washington tortillas that don't seem to taste ethnically authentic. I miss the Los Angeles dining experience, but it looks like it might be recaptured at this taco stand.

The Shilo Inn is easy to find. We just keep walking straight ahead until we hit the ocean. The Shilo chain is one of our favorites in the Pacific Northwest, and this hotel lobby is wonderfully oceanic, with a large aquarium that would rival some museums. But there's an unexpected problem – our room isn't ready for occupancy, although it's mid-afternoon.

No problem, we'll just wait here in the lobby. After a while, I wander towards the back of the hotel, where I find a comfortable TV room with no one in sight. The big-screen television is tuned to a news channel, so I play with the controls until I finally figure out how to change to the Olympics. Then I'm content to wait for as long as it takes to get the room ready.

Margy joins me a few minutes later. After an hour in front of the TV, she goes back to the front desk to ask about progress on the room. When she returns, she has a key.

"We've got a room, but we can't take our dog inside," she says.

"Eh?"

"That's what the delay was all about. The reservation was coded 'With Dog,' so that's why it took so long to get the room."

"I haven't seen a dog," I say.

"No. And now we have a deluxe room with a view, but no pets."

Once we get to our room, I'm content to watch more of the Olympics on TV, but Margy is in an exploring mood. So she goes to the beach while I become a couch potato. Along the shore, she finds a spot where huge kites are being flown.

Later, we walk back to the taco stand for a pleasant surprise. The little shed is wonderfully like the Southern California stands that serve outrageously delicious food. We order seafood tacos and churros, prepared to perfection. We eat them in one of the two small booths inside, and then order seconds.

That evening, we go for a walk down the main street parallel to the shore. It's getting dark, and there are no streetlights. Once again, the

Kites on beach at Ocean Shores

lack of a sidewalk forces us to walk in the road. It isn't a busy street, but I wonder how many tourists get bumped off by cars during the much busier summer season.

* * * * *

The weather forecast the next morning indicates the high-pressure system is finally breaking down. Although it should be clear all the way back to Bellingham, rain is expected by late tonight, so we get an early start, just in case.

We cruise past the Olympic Mountains in the smooth morning air, planning to make an intermediate stop at Arlington to replace the books that have been sold in the airport's bookstore. Margy closely checks our position on the VFR chart, though this part of Washington is becoming very familiar to us these days

.At Arlington, we discover the aviation bookstore is closed on Mondays, so our visit here has been somewhat futile. However, we can use the opportunity to fill up our gas tanks, in preparation for whatever adventure comes next.

Passing the Olympic Mountains, northbound

The self-serve pumps are a stumbling block once again. I can barely read the backlit credit card display in the bright morning light, but finally figure it out. Meanwhile, another airplane parks on the opposite side of the fuel island, and the pilot has at least as much trouble as I did when he tries to use the card reader. I watch him struggling with the display.

"Self-serve pumps always aggravate me!" I holler over to the pilot. "When I run for President, I promise to standardize all of them. Otherwise, we'll never figure these things out."

The other pilot laughs, but finally gets his credit card accepted, and I hear the pump start up.

"I wonder if it's like this in Seattle?" I yell over to him.

He shakes his head, indulging me, although I'm sure he doesn't have a clue what I'm talking about.

◊ ◊ ◊ ◊ ◊ ◊ ◊

Chapter 8

Heads-Up (Always)
Bellingham WA

ONE APRIL DAY, during a short stay in Bellingham, the weather turns good enough to fly. But time constraints raise their ugly head, so the best I'll be able to do is make a few solo circuits in the traffic pattern. The wind is gusty, but even if it looks too uncomfortable to work the pattern, I plan to take the Arrow out of the hangar and complete an engine inactivity run. Both the engine components and the pilot's neurons need frequent activity to keep their aviation tone.

When I arrive at the airport, the windsock is nearly straight out, but pointed almost directly down the runway. By the time the Arrow is out of the hangar and I'm in the cockpit and ready to start the engine, the wind has decreased in velocity, still from the south at about 15 knots.

I sit in the cockpit, and reach for the pre-start checklist in the side pocket. On the opposite end of the ramp, I notice preflight activity around one of the flight school's Cessna 172s. A Horizon Airlines turboprop taxis along the parallel taxiway, headed towards the terminal off to my right. Before the regional airliner disappears behind the hangars, an Allegiant Airlines MD-83 roars down Runway 16, taking off to the south. Bellingham Airport is like this – moments of extreme activity, followed by periods of quiet. I decide to wait for the quiet.

There's no hurry. I'm only going around the traffic pattern. In fact, I decide to let the Cessna 172 taxi out before me, although the two pilots (probably a flight instructor and student) are not yet in their airplane.

In a few minutes, the Cessna has its engine running, pauses in place for several more minutes, and then taxis toward the runway. This is a good time to start my engine.

I pull forward towards the self-serve fuel pumps, where I like to make my first contact with ground control. This gives me time to listen to the ATIS report of wind and airport conditions, while I position the Arrow where the control tower will be able to see it. Otherwise, the hangars block the tower's view.

"Bellingham Ground, Arrow Four-One-Niner-Niner-Seven, at the self-serve pumps, ready to taxi with Information Juliet."

"Arrow Four-One-Niner-Niner-Seven, taxi to Runway 16 via Delta, Alpha, Bravo."

I read back the taxi instructions, and pull forward toward Delta taxiway. The Cessna 172 has just started down the parallel taxiway, Alpha, at a pace a bit slower than normal. In my mind, I visualize a new student pilot, maybe on an introductory flight. Taxiing this slow is an sign this might be a training flight, and a few minutes ago I heard a very professional sounding female voice communicating with ground control. These two factors taken together indicate (to me) a new student and an experienced instructor. It's certainly not important to my situation, but I try to stay in tune with my surrounding environment when I fly, and this includes keeping an eye on nearby aircraft. Listening closely to other aircraft on frequency and watching airplanes as they progress around the traffic pattern pays dividends when it comes to awareness of your flying environment. Today, I'm paying even closer attention – solo takeoffs and landings under routine conditions should be no problem for me, considering my 7000 hours of flight time, but I'm about as noncurrent as I can get. Once the engine is running, I always feel more comfortable, but it's even more important to be sharply attentive when you've been away from the flight controls for a month.

Besides, Margy isn't here to back me up. It's a simple fact that two experienced pilots will look after each other closely, and Margy and I are a good team inside the cockpit. She's always quick to remind me when the transponder isn't properly set or I've added one notch of takeoff flaps rather than two for a short field takeoff. It's a big plus, especially when you're noncurrent. Today Margy's at home.

The communication frequency (ground control) is quiet now, with only the Cessna 172 and my Arrow in the movement area. There's no aircraft visible in the traffic pattern. The "quiet" I was hoping for couldn't get any better than this.

I soon catch up to the Cessna on Taxiway Alpha; so I slow down to provide increased spacing between us. The 172 peels off into the run-up area at the end of the runway (area Bravo), turns into the wind, and taxis far enough forward to allow room for me to pull into the wide paved area.

My run-up is thorough, but I finish before the Cessna. I pause just a few moments, waiting to see whether the other aircraft wants to go first, then pull out of the run-up area. Once again, my mental imagery shows an instructor and student thoroughly discussing their pre-takeoff checklist. As I switch to control tower frequency, I'm rolling slowly towards the runway hold-short line.

"Bellingham Tower, Arrow Four-One-Niner-Niner-Seven, holding short of Runway One-Six at Bravo, to remain in the pattern for touch and goes."

"Arrow Four-One-Niner-Niner-Seven is cleared for takeoff, Runway One-Six. Make right closed traffic. Report downwind each time."

"Four-One-Niner-Niner-Seven, cleared for takeoff. Right traffic, to report downwind."

All is quiet on tower frequency, and only the Cessna sits behind me on the ground. I like it this way.

After takeoff, I verify a positive rate of climb on the vertical speed indicator, and wait until mid-field before retracting the landing gear. It's seldom wise to retract the wheels with usable runway remaining. You never know when the engine might sputter.

Passing the end of the runway, I retract the flaps, reduce power to 25-25, and complete my climb checklist: mixture set at 12 gallons per hour, landing light and strobes on. Since I'll be downwind soon, I leave the electric fuel pump on.

At the shoreline, I turn right to fly the crosswind leg, check the airport profile behind my right shoulder, and then turn downwind. I keep my pattern in fairly close, arriving at traffic pattern altitude (1200 feet on the altimeter), just before reaching the abeam-the-tower reporting point. I lower the landing gear ("Three green," I call out loud), and make the necessary report: "Four-One-Niner-Niner-Seven, right downwind abeam, for touch and go."

"Arrow Niner-Niner-Seven, cleared touch and go."

"Cleared touch and go," I repeat, finishing my call with the Arrow's abbreviated call sign: "Niner-Niner-Seven."

Everything is so routine that it's almost scary. There's no one else on tower frequency, and the Cessna is still sitting in the run-up area. Again, I visualize the flight instructor giving her student pilot extensive last-minute instructions, making sure there are no surprises, which is a sign of thorough training.

I complete my landing checklist, calling out loud so there's no question in my mind: "GUMPS – gas on the left tank, which is fullest, with the pump; undercarriage three green; mixture full rich; prop full forward; seatbelts secured."

From inside the cockpit today, I can hear the distinct whistle that is a trademark of the Piper Arrow, a high-pitched sound caused by the wind flowing through the open wheel wells with the landing gear down. From outside, it's even more obvious, and any pilot below me knows an Arrow is inbound. Today, if I pay careful attention, I can hear the characteristic whistle from <u>inside</u> the airplane. Cool!

As I turn final approach, I make one last check of the two essentials that might still remain, and are never checked too often: "Three green with the prop." The air is soft and cooperating nicely, but I add 10 extra miles per hour for possible gusts – 100 miles per hour on final, rather than the standard 90. This is a long runway (for a Piper Arrow), so I can sacrifice a little pavement in exchange for a few knots of airspeed. This approach path traditionally includes gusts on short final, as aircraft cross Interstate 5 and the small ridge at the approach end of the runway. A little extra speed is a hedge for shifts in the wind that could be lurking there today. As I hit a minor gust and pass over the runway threshold, I notice the Cessna 172 is <u>still</u> in the run-up area.

Squeak, squeak. I'm down with a nice landing; main wheels first, the squeaks a little farther apart than perfect, but not bad for my first landing in a month. A few seconds later, the nose gear drops to the pavement with more of a *thunk* than a *squeak*, which is the way the Arrow's nose tire traditionally plops down.

"Flaps verified," I say out loud, retracting the flaps for the follow-through. I push the throttle forward, and continue with my touch and go. All is well, and it's extremely quiet on tower frequency. There's still only the tower controller and me, but the Cessna should be switching to our frequency for takeoff very soon.

The next circuit is identical, except now, as I turn final, I notice the Cessna pulling forward towards the runway hold-short line. I double-check that the 172 stops, and I'm expecting the flight instructor's first communication with the control tower any moment. As I approach the paved threshold and the Cessna slips behind my wing, I hear the instructor make her first call on control tower frequency – my frequency, where no one except the controller and I reside.

I'm ready to begin the flare now, a maneuver during landing considered the most crucial of all. With my considerable landing experience, it feels routine, a reassuring comfort. But when the flight instructor speaks, although her voice is calm and professional, she says something I've never heard before.

"Bellingham Tower, Cessna One-Seven-Two-Three-Delta sees two aircraft on final."

It's said calmly and clearly, but it makes no sense. Her initial call to the control tower should not involve traffic she sees in the pattern. Unless, of course, she's trying to get the control tower's attention to something that simply doesn't look right. I know there are no other aircraft the controller knows about in the pattern, or he would have been talking to them. And I know this is the right frequency, because I've been talking to the tower controller for the past 10 minutes, and now the Cessna is on the same frequency, as it should be. So if there's someone behind me on final approach, he shouldn't be there. This matter-of-fact report from the flight instructor sounds like an alert to the control tower.

So what should I do? I'm now in the mid-point of my flare for landing. In my Arrow, there's no way to see traffic directly behind me. And most importantly, if another airplane is really there, how close?

There's a lull of several seconds. Then the tower controller nearly screams into his microphone: "Eclipse Jet Seven-Four-Alpha, go around! Go around!" He pauses only momentarily, then again directs: "Eclipse Jet, go around immediately, go around!"

So now all is clear, although it makes no sense how this might have happened. A twin-engine private jet is behind me, way too close for comfort. And the jet has crept up on me, and has either not seen me or feels this is where he's supposed to be. Nothing makes sense!

I consider aborting my landing and starting an immediate climb. But that could pull me right into the path of a jet passing low and overhead. In the absence of more information or instructions from the tower controller, I do what seems best – I complete my flare carefully, and land, rolling down the runway centerline, ready to turn off at the first available intersection. Or should I continue with my touch and go, which was my last instruction from air traffic control?

It's suddenly dark, as the shadow of the jet passes directly over me, and then moves farther down the runway. The good news is the shadow is less than the runway width, so the jet is well above me now. Better yet, the shadow keeps moving forward and away from me. I crane my neck forward and up towards the top of the windshield. There it is – a twin-engine jet now climbing rapidly to the south.

The crisis is past, but it takes a while for everything to settle down. There are no voices on the frequency, so probably the controller is on another frequency trying to straighten things out, or maybe on the telephone, talking to Victoria Terminal, the controlling agency for IFR approaches to this airport. It seems fairly obvious that a missed handoff between Victoria and Bellingham is the culprit, only because nothing else makes sense. Even this isn't something anyone would expect (or accept).

Surely, the jet pilot has erred, since it would be impossible to appear on short final without a radio call to the control tower unless you've made a mighty big goof, no matter what any previous controller has told you to do. I use the quiet moments to add my two cents to the silent frequency, realizing the tower controller might be very busy. But I may be able to defuse things a bit.

"Bellingham Tower, would you like Nine-Nine-Seven to make this a full stop rather than follow through on the touch and go?"

It's a question that offers a small out for air traffic control. If I continue with my touch and go and go airborne again, I'll be climbing closer than normally allowed to a jet in front of me. However, from a safety point of view, I won't be closing on the jet as he speeds away. So there's no longer a concern for myself, but if I exit the runway, it would get one conflicting aircraft out of the system immediately.

No answer. So as I roll past the high-speed turnoff, I add power and follow through on my touch and go. I'm safely airborne again, and climbing nicely. I should be well clear of the departing jet's wake turbulence. In fact, he's now disappearing to the south, climbing like ..... well, like a jet. I continue a normal circuit, hopefully more routine than the last. When I turn crosswind, the tower controller finally breaks the silence, now sounding quite calm.

"Niner-Niner-Seven, Bellingham. Sorry I didn't get back to you on your last call. I was busy trying to close the Eclipse Jet's IFR flight plan. From where I sit, that was way too exciting."

"Mighty exciting from my seat, too," I answer.

"Cessna Two-Three-Delta, Bellingham. Sorry about the delay in your takeoff clearance. We'll get you out right away, but things have been a bit crazy."

You can say that again.

I want to intervene, and say something to the Cessna's instructor, like "Thanks!" But the Eclipse Jet hasn't yet reappeared in the traffic pattern, so things may still not be entirely under control. So I do the (seemingly) professional thing, and maintain my silence. I'm hoping, as things settle down, the tower controller will thank the Cessna for calling out the conflict before something really bad happened, like a Piper Arrow squashed on the runway with me inside. But the thank-you doesn't happen, and before I can intervene, the Cessna is cleared for takeoff, and the Eclipse Jet reappears, entering downwind in front of me, calmly talking to the tower, as if nothing has happened. Before I can thank the Cessna's instructor, she's gone.

Once the Arrow is back in the hangar, this gives me a lot to think about. I know a lot about air traffic control, and even more about piloting an aircraft. How such an event could have occurred can only be explained by multiple errors on the part of both the pilot and air traffic control. A jet moves plenty fast, and its pilot has to be far ahead of the aircraft. The Eclipse is a newcomer to the aviation field, one of the first jets designed for private use and licensed for single-pilot operations. A pilot with relatively little experience could legally fly this airplane without a copilot, including flight under instrument flight rules. It would make for a very busy cockpit, being heads-down with the instruments and charts a lot more often than is ideal.

Which is a good reason for all of us to always stay heads-up, even when flying around the traffic pattern on what seems the very quietest of days.

And Cessna Two-Three-Delta, if you're reading this – Thanks!

Center-of-Book Photos

Astoria, Oregon Runway 31

Winter at Bellingham, Washington

Fred Flintstone, Jr. and his dad (Adam)

Author (left) with Dale at Powell River, BC

Camping at Eastsound Orcas Island

N41997 on jacks during annual inspection

Orcas Island Runway 16

Bellingham Harbor and downtown, coming home

Jefferson County - Port Townsend, Wasington

Port Townsend cafe

Chapter 9

Rented Cop Cars
Newport OR

GENERAL AVIATION'S HEYDAY IS FAR BEHIND. Since the early 1980's, small aircraft have flown less and less, one of the biggest victims of economic declines. When the major global financial deterioration began in 2008, the number of private aircraft decreased even further. As older aircraft fell out of the inventory, few new airplanes replaced them.

On the other hand, little has changed for the American private pilot, who still has access to the freedom of the skies. Sure, gas prices are higher, but the overall escalation of the costs of flying is no more significant than price inflation in other recreational activities. The unconstrained environment aloft far outweighs the adverse affects of the private aviation industry's economic decline. I've seen both eras, and I still celebrate my freedom in the sky while recognizing that changes have been inevitable.

Exemplary of these trends is the ubiquitous two-seat Cessna 152, last produced in the 1980's. This airplane trained more new civilian pilots than any other aircraft in history. But as the last 152 rolled off the production line, student pilots slowly gravitated to larger four-place aircraft not originally designed as trainers. By the 1990's, most students were training in Cessna 172s and Piper Warriors. Today, it's hard to find a flight school with any 152s. Personally, I've logged more hours of right-seat time (what I call "riding time") in this aircraft than any other. As a flight instructor, the Cessna 152 has a special place in my flying heart.

During the decade of the last 152s, visits to small airports were especially appealing. Airport cafes, unlocked perimeter gates, and charming courtesy cars were the norm. In the case of Santa Ynez Airport in California, pilots flew there specifically for the thrill of driving one of the courtesy vehicles to the nearby Danish village of Solvang. Where else (at the end of the twentieth century) could you choose a car from a free fleet of classic 1958 Chevrolets?

Finding a courtesy car these days (to say nothing of an entire fleet) is less common. An exception is the friendly airport at Newport, Oregon. Things change fast at small airports as businesses and personnel change frequently (and not always for the better). This airport, however, has its act together, at least for now. And it's all set in a scenic ocean shore location, with a panoramic bridge across the bay.

Newport, Oregon

When Margy and I land at Newport, nothing has changed regarding the overall airport layout since our previous visits, except for one major addition – an active airport office. Margy flies the traffic pattern in perfect, no-wind conditions, touching down smoothly.

Our plan this morning is to refuel here, and then stop for lunch somewhere on our way home to Bellingham. The previous night, we camped at Siletz Bay, just to the north, but I'm now concerned with my decision regarding fuel reserves. We intentionally landed at Siletz Bay with reduced fuel, to keep our weight down for this morning's takeoff. A flight north to Astoria for avgas would have been okay, but it would definitely stretch our reserves. Newport, only a hop-and-skip to the south, was the obvious choice. From there, we can start back north with full tanks.

Back at Siletz Bay, earlier this morning, I called Olympia Airport to confirm their restaurant was still open. It's clearly designated in the Brown Book's airport diagram, right next to the control tower, but that means little these days. Airport cafes come and go with the tide, so it's best to call ahead.

When I dial the number for the cafe, it rings and rings with no answer and no voicemail. The reason seems obvious, but I decide to pursue it further by calling one of Olympia's fixed-base operators designated in the Brown Book.

"The restaurant closed a few months ago," says the woman who answers the phone. "Nothing else on the field."

"How about within walking distance?" I ask. "We're pretty good about hiking a mile or so for exercise."

"Nothing," she says. "But a fellow is talking about starting up the airport restaurant again. Maybe later this year."

Sounds promising for the future. Then again, probably not.

So now our revised plan is to gas up at Newport (no restaurant on the field), and continue north to Port Townsend, where we can eat at one of our favorite airport cafes. We might even make it in time for a late breakfast.

When we arrive at Newport, we taxi towards the ramp, and I'm typically displeased to find the increasingly common "Self-Service" sign. As usual, I'm prepared for the worst, but I try to stay optimistic as we ease in towards the pump.

"Maybe this self-serve will work better than others," I remark to Margy.

"Good news," she replies. "Here comes someone to help."

Sure enough, a jolly looking fellow is approaching the airplane. By the time our engine is shut down, he's waiting at the passenger door as Margy opens it.

"It's self-serve," he announces. (Pretty obvious, considering the sign.)

"Let me know if I can help," he adds. "The instructions on the pump should be simple to follow." (Not so obvious, but to think a real human being is here to lend assistance.)

"Thanks," says Margy. "We appreciate it."

"I'm Jimmy," he replies. "Anything else you need? I've got courtesy cars if you want to go to town."

"We were planning just to gas up and go," says Margy. "But we'll talk it over."

"If you want a car, just see me in the office. There are some good places to eat on the main highway."

My perpetual pessimism about airport self-service fuel pumps and the decade's general disappearance of customer service dissolves in an instant.

The next thing that happens is beyond belief. Jimmy steps in front of our Arrow, reaches down by the gas nozzle, pulls out a pair of gleaming, freshly painted chocks, and shoves them around our right main tire.

"Come see me before you leave," he says as he walks back to the office. "I'd like you to sign the guest book."

Guest book? Am I in a time warp?

* * * * *

THE OFFICE IS CLEAN AND COMFORTABLE, with cushy chairs and several piles of aviation magazines on the coffee table.

"We'll take you up on the offer of a courtesy car," I say to Jimmy. "We'll go to town for lunch."

"Okay, let me show you a map. There are quite a few places to eat."

He waves me over to the office counter, and pulls out a black-and-white map he (someone) has prepared just for visitors like us. Local tourist attractions are highlighted on the map, as are hotels and restaurants. Jimmy draws a circle around an unlabeled location.

Newport Airport office

"Personally, I like this place the best," he says. "Great breakfast, with 3-egg omelets. Right here on the northeast corner of this intersection."

Now this is getting crazy. How could Jimmy possibly know breakfast is my favorite meal, and omelets top my preferences. If it isn't a time warp, it must be some kind of weird dream.

Jimmy's recommendation sounds good, or we could eat at the Shilo Inn. I remember the restaurant at the hotel from an overnight stay a few years ago. On that visit, there was absolutely nobody at the airport when we arrived, and it was frustrating to phone a taxicab and wait for a much-delayed ride to town. On that trip, the quality of the Shilo made up for our frustrations upon arrival. Now this airport has a completely different feel.

The courtesy car is an old Crown Victoria, obviously a decommissioned police car. The vehicle is jet black with multiple antennas on the roof and a bench seat in front that seems huge. When I start the engine, it still has the vroom-vroom roar of a cop car.

Newport Airport Crown Vitoria courtesy car

It's a few miles to town, with a scenic entry via the big bridge looking down on the marina and the touristy part of town. We stick to the main highway, passing the Shilo Inn, following Jimmy's map towards the breakfast spot. But there's enough traffic that we miss a few intersection signs, and I think I've gone too far. I turn around at a small shopping center, and start back the other way. But we still don't see the restaurant, so we decide to simply continue until we reach the Shilo Inn.

Georgie's restaurant, adjacent to the hotel's lobby, is pretty much as I remember it – big booths, prompt service, and good food. Although breakfast is still being served, I can't pass up the delicious sand dabs I remember from my previous visit. Margy and I share a platter along with a salad, and it's plenty for both of us.

Leaving the hotel, I ask Margy whether we should get some gas for the Crown Vic.

"What's the gas gauge say?" she asks.

"Empty, but it was sitting on empty when we left the airport. The gauge probably doesn't work."

"Let's get some gas anyway," replies Margy. "It's fair to pay for what we've used."

So I pull into a no-name gas station with several long rows of pumps. This is Oregon, so self-serve for automobile gas (not airplanes) is prohibited. Jobs for Oregonians!

I order twenty dollars worth from the gas attendant, certainly a lot more than we've used. Then again, this Crown Vic probably guzzles gas, and we owe it to Jimmy. When the attendant returns to my car window to collect my cash, I notice him looking over the vehicle. I can't resist kidding him.

"Stolen cop car," I say, matter-of-factly.

"Oh!" says the young man.

We head back towards the airport, once again approaching the bridge. As the big Crown Victoria motors over the bridge and down the slope on the other side, a longhaired fellow is descending the walkway alongside the bridge. Probably because of the throaty sound of the Crown Vic, he looks back over his shoulder at us. When he sees our big black cop car coming, he steps toward the road, and points an outstretched arm at us with a pistol-grip gesture.

"Bang!" he yells as we pass by.

"Got me!" I yell.

I clutch a hand to my chest and make a deadly grimace. The man laughs.

"Must be Oregon," says Margy. "Just like the sixties."

Or maybe like the eighties.

The moral of the story is that you <u>can</u> go back in time. And when I'm in the area and need gas, I'll definitely stop at Newport. It's my hope Jimmy is still there, the Crown Vics are still around, and that management hasn't changed.

◊ ◊ ◊ ◊ ◊ ◊

Chapter 10

Airport Misguides
Scappoose OR and Chehalis-Centralis WA

PILOTS LOOKING FOR ADVENTURE routinely spend hours at home with aeronautical charts and airport guides, dreaming of places to fly. When time and weather permit, it's even more probable to find them pouring over their charts, considering where they want to go.

The aeronautical information available to us regarding safety-related items is, generally, accurate and up to date. But less critical data is not always current. An airport guide that identifies a cafe on the field can't be relied upon, particularly in troublesome economic times. And data about airports allowing (or encouraging) camping on the airport is tough to find. Which is one reason I tend to keep returning to my old standbys – airports where I've camped and found privacy and enjoyment, and restaurants I know are still open (at least on my most recent visit).

* * * * *

I SIT IN THE LIVING ROOM, using my laptop to Google a few prospective airports near Portland that seem logical spots for potential camping, but find little helpful data. Information about accommodations focuses on hotels, since that's what most pilots are seeking when it comes to lodging. (American Air Campers Association is an encouraging newcomer to the Internet world, a highly recommended paid subscription site for those who want to camp at their destination.)

Checking airports in the Brown Book reveals little about camping, although an airfield near Scappoose references a "campground adjacent," which probably means a major bag drag. If I can't camp next to my airplane, I'm inclined not to camp at all.

I flip the airport guide open to Kelso-Longview, since I vaguely recall seeing an entry there about camping on the field. If such an entry was published in the past, it's not in the latest edition of the guide.

Margy and I have planned a late afternoon departure, with our destination still to be decided. It's not unlike us to keep our route undetermined until after we're airborne. From Bellingham, most departures are to the south anyway, so we'll have time to discuss things as we settle into our climb. Besides, there's always Chehalis, an old standby for camping, or Siletz Bay if we're inclined to cruise farther south. Gas tanks to the tabs will be fine for either (Siletz Bay less so when headwinds prevail).

While Margy is doing errands in town, I pack a picnic supper from what I find in the refrigerator. I stuff a few items of extra summer clothing in my backpack, and grab a jacket just in case. Everything else we'll need is in the hangar – our camping gear stands by, always ready to go.

As for Margy, she left for her short journey around town with her backpack and whatever she needs for tonight, so she too is ready. Now it's just a matter of getting going. I dial up Margy on her cell phone.

"Meet me downstairs?" I ask, as soon as she answers.

"Be there in about 10 minutes. Just leaving the computer store now."

That's how simple it is. We're both used to departing on a moment's notice. The specific destination isn't critical, and we love to fly. So why should it be more complicated?

I'm standing by the elevator in the parking garage below our condo when Margy pulls in. Engine running, I hop into the passenger seat, and off we go.

"Have you decided where we're headed?" she asks.

"Not yet. How about south?"

"South would be good."

"Actually, I've looked at Scappoose," I note. "It's near Portland, just northeast a bit. Looks good, but I'm not sure if you can camp on the field. The Brown Book says 'camping adjacent,' whatever that means."

"Sounds promising," she says. "Control tower?"

"No, just a Unicom. But a nice, long paved runway."

Margy and I possess a natural compatibility that transfers nicely into the cockpit. We fly relaxed but attentive to items that might foster complacency regarding fight safety. An Arrow doesn't require two pilots, but we form the perfect advertisement for cockpit resource management, without taking the fun out of it.

* * * * *

CLIMBING OUT OF BELLINGHAM VFR, Margy flies while I set up the GPS route.

"Keep an eye out for traffic," I remind Margy. "I'll be heads-down for a few minutes."

"Sure. Is there a flight plan for Portland in the GPS?" she replies.

"Not exactly, but we'll fly the Port Townsend route for now, and I'll modify it to add Scappoose."

I've forgotten how to delete and add waypoints, another example of how keeping current makes information flow easier. But the quick-start manual for the GPS brings me up to date. I punch in Olympia and Chehalis, and then Scappoose.

Just to be sure about the camping situation at Kelso-Longview, I look up the airport information in the Brown Book. It's one edition newer than the copy back at the condo, but there's still no listing for camping on the field.

There's an old AOPA airport guide in the back seat, stored with the IFR charts. Even though it's not a current edition, sometimes it has more information about airport camping than the more elaborate books. So I take the time to dig out the oversized volume. Nothing about camping for either Kelso-Longview or Scappoose.

I double-check the GPS, which shows us directly on course for Penn Cove, with Olympia and Scappoose the next waypoints. Then I try setting the old Northstar (combined Loran-GPS) – never too many navigation backups – but I'm greeted by a "Memory Failed" message and an LED message: "May I change to GRI 9960?" It's an indication this ancient piece of equipment – 1990's technology already antiquated – is ready to be retired. The company has been out of business for a decade, and no software upgrades have been added since. GRI 9960 is the Northeast U.S. LORAN chain.

"Shall we navigate by Boston's LORAN stations?" I ask Margy.

"I'd rather not," she replies. "That thing never seems to work anymore."

"The database is so old it can't find the current satellite almanac, but usually the LORAN works. Acting crazy today. Maybe LORAN was decommissioned while we weren't paying attention."

(LORAN-C was still minimally operational at the time, but stations were already in the process of being withdrawn, one-by-one, and the navigation system disappeared from service in the U.S. a few months later in late 2010. With the increased reliability of GPS, LORAN was destined for the graveyard. When the complex of stations was operational, technicians were required at LORAN-C sites nearly full-time to keep the system functioning.)

By now, Margy is level at 7500 feet, a nice VFR cruising altitude for us. We'll navigate clear of the naval air station on Whidbey Island and outside of Seattle's Class B airspace, but we keep in contact with the controllers along the way. ATC almost never intervenes in our route of flight when flying VFR, but the traffic reports are always appreciated. And it's a good way to stay current on IFR en route procedures. In fact, once you're out of Bellingham's airport traffic area, there's little difference between IFR operations and VFR flight following in terms of communication and navigation procedures.

* * * * *

AN HOUR LATER, approaching Scappoose, Margy starts an early descent to give us a closer look at the area. It's a beautiful maze of water and land, dominated by the wide Columbia River.

My call to Scappoose Unicom goes unanswered, but a Cessna in the pattern offers an airport advisory – wind light and variable; he's the only known traffic. I take advantage of his hospitable voice to ask about camping on the field.

"There's a campground right next to the northwest parking area, with a man gate."

Columbia River near Scappoose, Oregon

"A what?" I say out loud on the intercom, without keying my microphone.

I glance at Margy, who is concentrating on entering the traffic pattern, and she's shaking her head – she doesn't understand either.

Turning final at Scappoose, Oregon

"Thanks. We'll check it out once we're on the ground," I reply over the radio.

When Margy turns onto final approach, I try looking for the campground, but can only see the parking area. It sits on the opposite side of the runway from the main line of buildings, next to a big hangar. This is a good sign, since it's on a remote corner of the airport, which is always preferred for camping. We don't need much – basically, a small clearing of grass near our wing will be fine. Or with our air mattress, even a paved ramp will do.

Once on the ground, Margy taxis to the parking area designated in our airport guide. There are no airplanes – only a large industrial-looking hangar with closed doors and a tall fence with a small personnel gate – a "man gate."

"Oh, so that's a man gate," I say to Margy.

"Exactly what he said. Weren't you listening," she kids.

We pull up near the corner of the paved ramp, farthest from the hangar. Right here would be a perfect place for us to camp, but it's not a designated camping area. The hangar seems totally inactive (at 5 o'clock), so why not just pitch our tent? Beyond the man gate is the commercial campground, all RV's as far as I can determine, and way too crowded.

"Let's camp right here," I say, as soon as the engine stops.

"We should take a look at the campground," replies Margy.

There's a lot unsaid in this statement. I feel better about stretching rules than Margy. I recall a similar instance at Shelter Cove Airport in California. We tried to camp next to our airplane there, with a commercial campground a few hundred feet away. We just finished setting up our tent when a voice blared over the campground loudspeaker: "Will the people with the airplane please move their tent into the official camping area!" Anything for a buck, even if the consumer doesn't need a real campground. Needless to say, we moved our tent into the Shelter Cove campground, disgruntled about being crammed in among big RVs.

We leave our camping gear behind, and walk through the man gate to the camping area. This entails hiking a half-mile down the road to get to the campground's entrance. I look over the terrain, trying to figure how we can make a shortcut by cutting directly across to the campsites, but there's a large ditch and a fence in the way. Inside the campground, I can see a children's playground, numerous dogs, and large RVs. I have nothing against kids, dogs, or RVs, but this place isn't for us.

"Let's go back," I say. "I don't see why we can't just camp next to our airplane. There's nobody around."

"I don't feel right about it," says Margy.

"Then let's just walk back to our airplane for now."

By the time we get back to the Arrow, we'll both have thought things through a little more, which is a good thing.

When we arrive at the plane, the grassy spot next to the Arrow looks even better to me than it did when we arrived. Meanwhile, a man has appeared in a lawn chair, on the airport side of the man gate, relaxing there for no apparent reason and cuddling a small dog between his legs.

In an unusual act of extrovert behavior (for me), I walk over and start a conversation. I introduce myself with what I think is a humorous statement.

"I was hoping I could temporarily promote you to airport manager to help me with a decision," I say.

"Well, you sure picked the wrong guy," he replies with a friendly laugh. "Me and Charlie are just sitting here watching airplanes takeoff and land."

"I was wondering what you think would happen if we pitched a tent next to our airplane for the night."

"You mean like a circus tent?"

I haven't misjudged. There's something about a guy in a lawn chair cuddling a dog near a man gate that makes me comfortable.

"No, no. Just a little tent. But I'm not sure we'd get arrested or something."

"Arrested? I doubt it. But I'm not sure about those people who run the trailer park."

Trailer park. That's what it looks like. To call it a campground is a bit of a misnomer.

"Do you know anything about them? Or about the airport policy?" I ask.

"Not really. It looks fine to me, but I'm certainly not the airport manager."

In the end, I decide it's not worth worrying about. And I don't want Margy to worry either, so I offer a suggestion to her.

"Why don't we get out of here? How about Chehalis?"

"Sounds fine to me. There's plenty of sunlight left."

It's great to have an amiable co-pilot.

* * * * *

ON THE FLIGHT TO CHEHALIS, we pass almost directly over Kelso, so I consider trying to find someone on the radio to talk to about camping on the field. We've camped many times at Chehalis, and a change of pace would be nice. But my calls to Kelso-Longview Unicom go unanswered, and no one is in the traffic pattern to provide airport information, so we simply press on.

This flight, technically, is Margy's flight review. As her flight instructor, it's perfectly legal for me to sign off a flight review every 24 months, and this multi-leg cross-country flight is perfect for the task. Officially, per the FARs, it's not possible to fail a flight review. However, a flight instructor can refuse to sign off a flight review due to inadequate performance, requiring the pilot to approach another flight instructor (or the same one) for another flight review.

This all applies, of course, to pilots who fly with flight instructors who are not their spouse. In fact, I confess to the fact that I sometimes tell Margy after a seemingly routine flight that she just completed her flight review. On the other hand, a "seemingly routine flight" is the perfect excuse for signing off a pilot for this every-other-year requirement. Although flight reviews typically include an approach and departure stall and a few other training maneuvers, no regulation dictates such actions. The major thing a good instructor is looking for on a flight review is solid ("routine") mastery of the flight.

In this instance, I've told Margy in advance this overnight trip will be her flight review. I don't notice her shaking in her boots. Still, she doesn't offer me the controls as we approach Chehalis, which I take as an indication she's striving to prove her skills.

The landing at Chehalis is just what a flight instructor looks for – stable on final approach, with full flaps, a comfortable rate of decent, and little need to adjust the throttle. But contrary to the reported weather on the AWOS recording, the wind is not right down the runway. Instead the winds are gusting side-to-side, and you can feel the Arrow being tossed around on short final. I watch Margy take charge of the situation, forcing the airplane into alignment with the runway, adding a touch of power for the gusts, and beginning the flare at exactly the right time. But winds can make a fool of any pilot, and our airspeed starts to decay rapidly when we're only a few feet above the pavement. Bam! We whack down on the runway perfectly aligned and totally safe, but certainly not smooth.

"Just find another instructor, and try to get him to sign you off!" I kid, as we rollout down the runway.

Margy laughs, but knows she did the best she could in the

Camping at Chehalis Airport, Washington

circumstances. As I often remind her, the safest landing isn't always the smoothest. Both of us have flown enough to know the truth in this statement. Alignment of the longitudinal axis straight down the runway with the main gear touching before the nose wheel is of prime importance. And that describes her landing. By comparison, smoothness barely counts.

Once we're parked in the airport camping area adjacent to the self-serve gas pumps, it's a pleasure to set up our tent for the night. This is one of the nicest camping areas we've ever encountered, and we keep returning again and again.

There are several picnic tables, and the restrooms are among the cleanest you'll find in any campground. On this visit, the adjacent building is under renovation, a victim of the recent winter floods that wreaked havoc on this area, leaving distinct water marks four-feet-high on the outside of the structure. This major event necessitated evacuation of airplanes from the airfield and a complete shutdown of Interstate 5 running next to the airport. Travel between Seattle and Portland was disrupted for a full week.

We eat our picnic dinner, and enjoy the sunset. With twilight still lingering, we climb into the tent, turn on our reading lights, and enjoy the cool evening air. As I linger on the pages of my book, growing increasingly tired, I need to reread some of the paragraphs for comprehensive, which is an indication I'm quickly slipping into sleep. A little girl speaks with a high-pitched tingle of excitement.

"Hello, campers!" she says in a not-too-loud voice, probably warned by her mother or father of the late hour.

"Hello, out there!" I reply.

I smile as I imagine a young girl walking with her parents, past a variety of airplanes at a charming airport, enjoying the evening glamour of a quaint, personable airport. Look – there's people camping next to their airplane!

I put down my book, turn out my light, and enjoy the feeling of being totally relaxed as I drift off to sleep. But a few hours later, I awaken, and have to think for a moment to remember where I am. It seems a bit bright inside the tent for night on an airport. The rotating beacon sweeps by, and the top of the tent brightens even more in a sudden splash. But that flit of light is well above the ground, and it shouldn't have awakened me. Instead, the entire inside of the tent seems engulfed in a murky brightness.

I slide out of my sleeping bag, and open the tent zipper. A nearly full

Full moon at Chehalis Airport, Washington

moon hovers over Chehalis. Can there be a national park campground experience more splendid than this?

* * * * *

THE NEXT MORNING, Margy and I walk across the street to the golf course for breakfast, then over to the airport office near midfield, a new building on a raised platform that should weather the next major flood. We talk with Allyn, the young airport manager who is a graduate of Bellingham's Western Washington University. I ask about the flood marks on the building near the camping area.

"The flood was quite an experience," he says. "Where you are camped now, the top of your tent would be underwater."

I leave a copy of my first aviation book, *Up the Airway (Coastal British Columbia Stories)*, in the lounge area near Allyn's office. The only other person in the building, apparently a local pilot, immediately picks up the book. I ask him where he's from.

"Toledo, down near Portland," he says. "I work at the skydiving center there."

"We're from Bellingham," I reply. "Part-time there, and part-time in Canada."

"I heard you mention you're camping," he says. "You should try Toledo, near Kelso. You can camp on the field. It's in all of the airport guides."

Chapter 11

Experimental Mecca and Oil Dipsticks
Arlington WA

THE EXPERIMENTAL AIRCRAFT ASSOCIATION is headquartered at Arlington Airport, 50 miles south of Bellingham. Every summer, the EAA holds their annual fly-in and airshow. Recreational flyers from all over the U.S. (Canada, too) wing their way to this airport to see the latest in home-built aircraft and to share their aviation enthusiasm with each other. It's a great event where you can camp by your airplane and spend some time enjoying the comaraderie.

Two decades ago, Margy and I flew north from our home in Los Angeles on our typical summer vacation to Canada, overnighting first in Oregon, and then at Arlington for the airshow weekend. In Grants Pass, our previous stop, we purchased two bottles of Oregon wine, wrapped some of our spare clothes around them to prevent the glass bottles from breaking during flight, and packed the wine away for later consumption.

At Arlington, we enjoyed a great Friday night barbecue with fellow pilots, all of us awaiting the next day's aviation displays and flight demonstrations. Arlington is that kind of place, any time of the year – a wonderful airport with character.

When we returned to our tent that evening, we began to unpack our meager bags, but there was no need to unwrap the wine. We'd forgotten this was quality wine (the corked variety), and liquids under pressure at altitude have a habit of popping corks. Our clothes were soaked and wreaking with fine wine.

Margy washed our clothing in a nearby sink, and I draped them over our traditional Arrow clothesline (the wire ADF tuning antenna running from the top tail to the roof of the cockpit). Tacky airplane campers!

That's often how lessons are learned – the hard way. And lessons about operating aircraft are sometimes learned the same way. "Better safe than sorry" is an even better method, if you can adhere to it. The wine incident is a reminder that everything about flight in an airplane must be thought through carefully.

* * * * *

"It's not a Monday," notes Margy, as she looks over the Seattle sectional chart in the living room.

I know exactly what she means, since I've just asked her if she has any ideas about where we should fly today. It's a fair-weather August day, and any destination will be fine for both of us, but it should be fairly close, since we need to be home by early evening.

"Sure," I reply. "Arlington will be fine."

We've been trying to get to Arlington for months. My Canadian aviation book, *Up the Airway*, is out of stock at Arlington's pilot shop where Jan and Rick support my publishing efforts by selling my books on consignment. Jan is always quick to send me a check when she sells a copy of the book, exactly the kind of vendor a small publisher appreciates. But every time we've dropped in to restock the books, it's been a Monday. The pilot shop is closed on Mondays. But today is a Friday.

Friday is also a good day to visit Arlington for other reasons. This busy airport can be chaotic on Saturdays and Sundays, when the experimental airplanes based there (gliders, also) take to the sky in droves, some of them without radios (or refusing to use them). Personally, I prefer a nice tower-controlled airport rather than a field with a Unicom. I'm pleased to be regulated, in return for a sense of controlled traffic flow. On the other hand, some of the greatest airports in the world are uncontrolled, so get over it, Wayne.

Our departure from Bellingham is routine, although the airport is undergoing extensive reconstruction. For now, there's substantial taxiway work during the daytime, resulting in circuitous routes to the runway, but well-supervised by Ground Control. Runway work is relegated to middle-of-the-night hours, when the airport is temporarily closed. Later this month, the airport will be completely closed for two weeks while the runway is overhauled. How many air carrier airports in the nation are completely closed for any extended period of time? Answer: Bellingham.

Today we're directed to Runway 16 for departure, on and off parallel taxiway Alpha and past huge earthmovers crossing our path: "Caution for equipment crossing the Taxiway Alpha," warns the control tower.

As we taxi, dust swirls around the Arrow. At the end of the runway, more excavation equipment is lined up off to the side, ready for the middle-of-the-night operations on the runway itself.

The VFR flight to Arlington is short and simple. A direct route keeps us out of Whidbey Island's airspace, so we don't talk to anyone after leaving Bellingham. Margy flies while I play with the GPS and do an inflight dual-VOR check for the logbook. I test one navigation radio against the other to assure they meet the 30-day IFR check criteria of no more than 4 degrees difference between receivers.

Listening to the Unicom at Arlington, it's apparent aircraft are using Runway 34, which sets us up well for a 45-degree entry to left downwind. But everyone is stepping on everyone else on frequency, caused by a sudden mass of aircraft in the pattern. It may be mid-day Friday at Arlington, but it feels like a Sunday.

Besides the normal traffic, there's a warbird jet fighter doing an overhead break for a low pass. Meanwhile a helicopter is operating off Runway 29, and a glider has reported an approach to final on the grass strip between the paved taxiway and Runway 34 where we'll land. To Arlington pilots, it's probably just another typical day. To me, it's a mess.

"Keep your eyes open," I say. "I'll do the landing if you help me watch for traffic."

It's an obvious statement. Margy is good about maintaining constant vigilance for other traffic, and she does her job well today.

"There's one in front of us, just entering downwind on the forty-five," she reports. "And another about to depart on Runway 34."

Although it's busy, we fit into the traffic without needing to modify our arrival in any way. When we're downwind abeam the numbers, everything has settled down, and the Unicom frequency grows silent. Just as we turn final approach about a mile out, a single-engine Cessna touches down on Runway 34.

Runway 34, Arlington, Washington

"Should have plenty of space between us," says Margy. "The Cessna's turning off the runway now. But there's an airplane and glider on the grass between the runway and parallel taxiway, waiting for takeoff. Plus the glider that just landed – he's stopped now, at the end of the grass strip."

The grass area is where gliders are towed upward, and where they land in a right traffic pattern that supposedly keeps them separated from powered aircraft in the left-hand pattern. But I've flown gliders before, and I know how limited they are without an engine during landing. They do what they need to do when they need to do it.

Once on the ground, I make the first turnoff that our speed permits. We land short enough to taxi behind the approach end of the grass strip, and I'm glad when we're on the parallel taxiway, headed for the pilot shop.

The building is primarily an aviation bookstore, a cute little shop near the self-serve gas pumps. It's like a trip back in time. Or at least it has always been this way on our previous visits. But this time, as we pull past the self-serve island, something is astray. The small pilot shop looks dark and quiet, unlike our previous visits.

"Looks closed," says Margy.

"Oh, no, we should have known," I reply.

Why we should have known is more because of the aviation economy than the obvious quality of the shop and its products. The global financial downturn begun in 2008 is now two years old, but airport businesses had been floundering well before the rest of the world recognized financial near-collapse.

I pull around the fuel pumps and into a parking spot that seems satisfactory for transient aircraft, although unmarked, and shutdown the Arrow. This looks like a good place to stop and explore the airfield.

Before setting off on foot from the parking ramp, I unlatch the oil filler access panel, and unscrew the dipstick, letting it rest on the edge of the filler tube, which allows the oil system to vent some of its hot, acidic fumes. Then I close the access latch. This has become standard procedure for us in recent years, since I'm convinced getting rid of crankcase gases is one of the keys to engine longevity. It's a simple ritual to follow, recommended to me by one of the nation's experts in aircraft engine care when I was privileged to talk with him several years ago.

The only potential problem with this procedure is failure to secure the oil dipstick before the next flight, which is a significant concern. However, there would never be a time when Margy or I wouldn't check the oil level before flight, even during a quick turnaround anywhere we might fly. So the possible danger is easily dismissed, and we've lived successfully with this procedure for years.

We explore around the old pilot shop, finding a completely vacant establishment. It's sad to see this previously joyful place in such an inactive state.

"Well, let's see if we can find somewhere to eat," I say.

We've heard that the main restaurant on the airport recently went out of business, but maybe there's someone new trying to get a cafe started. Around airports, there's always somebody trying to make a fresh start. These are places where dreamers and pragmatists exist side-by-side.

Considering the size of this airfield and its many businesses, aviation and otherwise, there's certainly a population big enough to support a restaurant. Pilots, mechanics, and airport lovers are always looking for a place to congregate and spend their money on lunch or just coffee.

In fact, as we taxied in today, we saw a promising sight – a flightline restaurant halfway down the field from the old pilot shop. It certainly looked open: "I think I even see people inside," reported Margy as we taxied past. But maybe this was the old restaurant that had gone out of business.

As soon as we begin walking towards the prospective restaurant, a banner on the side of a building catches my eye. The sign is on the street paralleling the airport, well away from the restaurant we noticed while taxiing in. The banner reads: *Flying J Cafe*.

"Do you think it's open?" I ask Margy, gesturing towards the building.

"Maybe, but it's hard to tell from here."

"Let's walk down to the big restaurant first. If it isn't open, we can try this place."

We follow the shoulder of the taxiway, past hangars exhibiting indications of airport prosperity. Mixed into the environment are buildings housing businesses that seem to have no aviation connection, industrial-looking concrete structures accessible only from the street. There's a blend of hefty locked gates leading to airport taxiways, contrasting with other spots where meager barbed wire or no fence at all parallels the street. It's hard to find airports these days with free access, but this one seems to be public-friendly in many spots. Maybe there's still hope for kids who stand outside airports, staring at the ramp, hoping for an invitation to look at airplanes. Not since September 11, 2001, has this experience been universally available to children. It's a big loss for our nation.

We pass a picnic table and horseshoe pit near a closed hangar, and then a big twin-engine previous-military C-46, olive drab in color. This aircraft needs lots of work, including replacement of a missing right-hand elevator. The bulky wings are roped to huge barrels filled with water that act as tie-downs. The old aircraft looks rather permanent here, but it's parked right in the middle of one of the prominent ramps, blocking access to the inner taxiways.

At another picnic table alongside the hangar adjacent to the C-46, five men are talking with animated hand gestures that I imagine have something to do with this immense restoration project. Airport people are often visionary romantics willing to spend enormous sums of money on remotely prospective projects, and sometimes it even works out.

Hints that food and drink are topics of interest are everywhere in this area. One sign says: *Flight Instruction and Espresso*. Another sign says simply: *Eats*, with an arrow pointing towards a small hangar. But the *Eats* sign has the logo of a steaming cup of coffee in the corner, indicating the "Eats" might be limited to donuts.

We pass a ramp lined with trailers containing gliders with their wings removed. Soaring is a major operation at this airport, but today we only see two operating from the grass strip, the gliders that got our attention during landing.

There are more picnic tables along this portion of the ramp, which causes me to make a sarcastic remark to Margy: "Maybe this is an airport where you're supposed to bring your own food."

When we finally reach the big restaurant, things look promising. A neon beer sign in the window glows red.

"There's definitely someone moving around inside," says Margy. "Oh, oh, look at that."

She points to a small sign we can now read at this close distance: *Open 7:30 to 2:30*.

"What time is it?" I ask.

Margy glances at her watch, and gives me a twisted-lip expression.

"Two-thirty-eight," she replies.

"Figures. So close, yet so far."

"Almost made it," she replies. "I guess Arlington pilots don't eat dinner."

We hike back along the ramp, inspecting one of the open hangars, walking inside where a spotless Pitts Special is parked. No one is anywhere in sight.

Then we come to the line of hangars where we saw the cafe banner. As we walk down the row towards the street, we hear a screen door slam. Someone is coming out of the cafe!

The *Flying J Cafe* is a great find. I polish off a tasty chunk of meatloaf, while Margy enjoys an egg salad sandwich.

* * * * *

When we're ready to depart Arlington, I open the Arrow's oil access door and check the dipstick – almost 7 quarts, ready to go. I check the fuel tanks, and they're just below the tabs, as expected. A quick walk around the aircraft is all that's necessary, since we landed less than 2 hours ago.

Margy goes through the engine-start checklist, and begins to taxi to Runway 34. Halfway to the run-up area, she provides one of her typically insightful comments.

"You screwed the oil dipstick back in, didn't you?"

"Yes," I reply. "I checked the oil – 7 quarts."

Conclusion: if you check the oil level, you obviously screw the dipstick back in. The access panel, which is right in front of me on my side of the windshield is latched closed, another means of confirming all is well. Or is it?

I don't actually remember screwing the dipstick back in, but I do remember checking the oil level and closing the access panel. So the dipstick must be firmly in place.

"Even if the dipstick was loose, it wouldn't be a problem," I suggest. "Unless you did extreme maneuvers or flew upside down, the dipstick would just rattle around a bit."

"Wouldn't we vent some oil?" she asks.

"Don't think so. And if we did, it would show up on the windshield as a warning before we lost too much oil. The crankcase isn't pressurized."

This is what's known as rationalization. I've adequately convinced Margy, but I'm not sure I've convinced myself.

As Margy turns the aircraft around at the end of the taxiway to face into the wind for run-up, I hear a minor rattle I can't identify.

"Do you hear that clanging noise?" asks Margy.

So she heard it, too. Not unusual, of course. A metal airplane is subject to lots of minor rattles that mean nothing. It could be as simple as a chart clip rubbing against the yoke. But this minor noise seemed to come from the engine compartment. The rattling noise stops.

"I heard it, too, but it's gone now," I say. "Let's see what happens during run-up."

Margy nods in acceptance of this routine noise. During throttle increase, everything rattles a little, but a loose dipstick should be easily distinguished. Maybe.

Run-up is normal. The mags check out fine, the prop cycles smoothly, and all gauges are right where they should be. And no unusual noises.

I wait for Margy to complete her pre-takeoff checklist. But I now recognize the obvious – it would be totally negligent to proceed with the takeoff when there's a possibility the dipstick is loose. We've got lots of time, and there's no one else in the run-up area. In a matter of just a few minutes, we could shut the engine down and check the dipstick. The only problem with this scenario is it's abnormal, and that's when you can make mistakes. So I let Margy complete her checklists and then explain what I want to do.

"Okay, how about going through the shutdown checklist now, and I'll check the oil dipstick. Just in case."

Margy is quick to nod agreement. The shutdown is simple, just a matter of turning off all the electrical subsystems, pulling the mixture lever to idle-cutoff, killing the master switch, and turning the magnetos off.

When the prop swings to a stop, I exit the airplane and open the oil access panel. The dipstick is firmly in place.

"The dipstick was screwed in," I say to Margy as I take my seat beside her in the cockpit.

"Better safe than sorry."

She's right. And I'm glad I took the time to be 100 percent sure.

"If you don't mind, I'll go through the re-start," I tell Margy. "A true hot start."

While Margy runs the engine start checklist for me, I set the engine controls appropriate for a hot start, a procedure in an Arrow that's a bit clumsy and not always successful: electric fuel pump on, but no prime; throttle full forward and mixture full aft. I crank and crank and crank. The engine sputters and finally fires. I quickly push the mixture forward and pull the throttle back to idle, and the motor begins to run smoothly.

"The curse of fuel injection," I say.

And it is a bit of a curse. Hot starts in this engine are finicky. I've been known to kill the battery under similar circumstances. If you're going to stop for lunch, fine – the engine will usually cool enough to provide a normal start an hour later. But a shorter period between shutdown and restart can be an agonizing experience with a fuel injected Lycoming.

Margy completes the pre-takeoff checklist, does a 360 clearing turn in the run-up area to check for traffic in the pattern, and pulls up to the runway hold line.

"Ready?" she asks.

"Ready," I reply. "Dipstick included."

I make the radio call announcing our departure. Home we go, better safe than sorry.

◊ ◊ ◊ ◊ ◊ ◊

Chapter 12

South on Victor 27

Washington, Oregon, and California

FAVORITE AIRPORTS ARE PLENTIFUL in a pilot's mind, and favorites sometimes change over time. Often it's an unusual once-in-a-lifetime airport that lingers in our thoughts. Another kind of favorite is an airport you return to again and again to take advantage of the routine you've enjoyed for years. You can't fly near favorite airports without dropping down and visiting. For me, Siletz Bay is such a place.

This is a perfect camping destination – a low-activity strip with plenty of paved runway, sea level density altitude, and right along my often-traveled route from Washington to California, Victor 27. I've never visited this airport when any other campers were present, although there's a nicely developed campsite in the woods right behind the parking ramp. It's an easy walk from the parking ramp, but my preference is camping right next to my airplane. Avoiding a bag-drag is a bit lazy, but it's more than that. There's something very personal about putting your tent up right beside your most-cherished machine. (Even <u>under</u> your wing, for those with high-wing aircraft, but watch out for those fuel vents!)

Siletz Bay is the perfect flying distance from Bellingham (less than three hours), a good first night out when heading south to California. When returning north, it can be reached from Los Angeles after one fuel stop on a long summer day. This airport often fits into my coastal travels. It also serves as a simple out-and-back overnight camping trip from Bellingham. I never tire of a trip to Siletz Bay.

Siletz Bay Airport, GlenEden Beach, Oregon

* * * * *

SUMMER MOVES IN, but I'm tied up with publishing projects. Besides, during my stays in Bellingham, the weather fights me. Mornings that are below my personal minimums seem more common during my trips to Bellingham from Canada. I shouldn't be surprised. This summer, I've enjoyed glorious days at my floating cabin on Powell Lake. The tradeoff isn't forced on me, since I often return to Bellingham during periods when the weather turns sour, seldom missing stunningly sunny days on Powell Lake. My flying proficiency suffers from this international travel pattern, and so does the Arrow's engine activity. Since the annual inspection last autumn, the airplane has accumulated only 20 hours. So I schedule a dramatic fix for the situation – a solo round trip to Los Angeles.

Summer flights to California have been a regular part of my routine. But in the past, they have been combined with lots of local flying activity near Bellingham. This trip will be undertaken after a bout of extended flight inactivity for both the Arrow and me. Most unusual of all, I'll make the flight solo.

Of my thousands of hours in this airplane, only a few of them have been alone. Having Margy in the other seat is an obvious luxury. Sharing the excitement of flight together is a thrill enhanced by the benefit of an extra pilot up front to relieve the workload. In a nutshell, I've been spoiled by thousands of hours of relying on Margy to keep the wings level, precisely targeted on heading and altitude, while I play with the navigation radios and charts, allowing me to comfortably talk to ATC. I've always appreciated her presence on cross-country flights, especially her mental reinforcement regarding inflight decisions. Over time, solo flights have become less frequent for me, and I don't miss the experience.

Thus, I launch on this exciting flight with a bit of trepidation. I'm confident, but bordering on non-current and without my dependable co-pilot. Of course, I do have George, my trusty autopilot, and a rare opportunity to fly from the left seat. In the past, when I've conducted solo flights in this airplane, I've almost always flown from the right seat, where I feel most comfortable. But on a long flight like this, it seems logical to put myself in front of the flight instruments on the left side. I should quickly adjust to the change of position. It's just a matter of different hands on the yoke and throttle, enhanced by flight information right in front of me. I linger on this decision for awhile, wondering if the adjustment is worth the better visibility of the instruments. It seems a moot point, since I always feel comfortable in the right seat, but I finally decide to make the flight from the other side of the cockpit.

I depart Bellingham on September 21st, the last official day of summer, with extensive good weather stretching all along the Pacific Coast. This is a flight I'm used to completing in two days, or even in a one-day sprint (10 to 11 hours of flight, with two fuel stops). This time of year, days are getting shorter, so I plan to make several overnight stops. Plus, I want to enjoy the luxury of camping by my airplane, and there's no hurry to get to Los Angeles. One of my goals is to visit some new airports, maybe even bypassing Siletz Bay for a change.

On my takeoff roll at Bellingham, I feel uncomfortable. It's severe clear with no wind, but I'm solo in the cockpit and in the left seat for the first time in nearly a decade. The yoke feels awkward in my left hand, and I can't get a comfortable grip on the throttle with my right. Everything seems amazingly backwards.

I flounder a bit on the centerline, but rotate fairly precisely. Once airborne, as is common on almost all flights, everything settles down quickly. The familiarity factor comes into play as I retract the landing gear and establish standard 25-25 climb-out settings for manifold pressure and prop speed. The flight instruments feel close and intimate from the left seat, and George is standing by to assist me during the climb. I take advantage of his support by clicking the autopilot on. Now I can relax and scan more thoroughly for traffic during the climb-out. All is well, but flying still feels a bit strange from this side of the airplane.

By the time I cross over Olympia, I'm feeling better in the left seat. Of course, George is doing all of the flying. The attitude indicator (technically, the flight command indicator, since it's part of the flight director) and HSI are right in front of me, and seem almost too close for comfort. But I should be fully relaxed before I arrive at Ocean Shores on the Washington coast. This runway is only a little shorter than Siletz Bay, where I always feel comfortable. Plus, I'm lighter today than any cross-country flight with Margy and all of our baggage. The aircraft will perform admirably at this sea-level airstrip during takeoff, and landings are an aspect of flight that almost always feels comfortable to me. But maybe not from the left seat.

I turn westward, cross the last major ridge before reaching the coast, and begin a VFR descent. I'm navigating direct to Hoquiam Airport, with plans to overfly this large uncontrolled field, and then fly direct to Ocean Shores, where I plan to camp beside my airplane rather than hike to the hotel in town. Since I'll be overflying Hoquiam, why not use this airport's long runway as a spot to practice a few landings from the left seat? It seems logical to regain my currency on a forgiving runway before attempting a landing on a smaller strip. There's lots of daylight left, and nothing to rush me to my camping destination, so better safe than sorry.

I descend south of Hoquiam and enter on the forty-five, downwind for right traffic on Runway 6. With no one in the pattern, this is an ideal place to practice takeoffs and landings. But there's irony in the fact that a 7000-hour pilot needs to practice landings before tackling the well-within-limits 2700-foot runway at Ocean Shores. Lack of currency and left seat discomfort take their toll.

It's a decision well worth my time and effort. After three touch-and-goes, I'm much more confident about tackling Ocean Shores. My landings and follow-throughs are precise and smooth, but still a bit uncomfortable, considering the different angle of view over the cowling from the left side. Surely, being left-seat-shy will pass quickly on a trip all the way to Los Angeles. Then again, maybe not.

After my third landing, I climb out downwind, and head direct to Ocean Shores. I make a multicom call to report my position and intensions, planning to overfly the small runway to check the windsock. Based on the light wind at Hoquiam, I expect to land to the south at Ocean Shores, but I'd like to look the airport over first. Not unexpectedly, the frequency is quiet. I make another report of my position approaching the airport, a short flight of only a few minutes from Hoquiam.

Just as expected from my review of the airport chart and my previous visit with Margy, the runway has wide-open approach zones, but the activity at the small airstrip is definitely not what I expect. A pickup truck is driving down the runway, and big white X's are positioned on both ends of the landing strip.

Of course, I always check NOTAMs before flight, even in severe-clear VFR conditions. Don't you?

I overfly the airport, and report my position and intensions on the radio in case the workers below are nervous about my arrival overhead while they're working: "Ocean Shores Traffic, Arrow Niner-Niner-Seven is over the airport, departing the area to the south."

Suddenly, the hours of sunlight are a factor. It takes only a few seconds to select a good alternate under the circumstances – Siletz Bay.

I climb back up to 6500 feet, check in with Seattle Center for VFR flight following, and head direct to Astoria. Just the thought of landing at Siletz Bay makes me feel comfortable, even from the left seat.

Travelling towards Astoria, and then down Victor 27, produces an element of familiarity that improves my spirits. The coast is sparkling clear, and both Astoria and Tillamook are reporting light surface winds from the northwest, ideal conditions for a landing at Siletz Bay.

South of Tillamook, I cancel flight following with Seattle Center and begin my descent towards Siletz Bay. I flow smoothly into the downwind leg for a landing to the north. My path tracks just offshore, paralleling the familiar runway.

I'm prepared for the downdrafts on short final that seem to always lurk here. They arrive right on schedule, bouncing me around a bit, and then right back onto an acceptable glide path. I touch down and rollout smartly on centerline, as if I were in the right seat. The result is flawless, but the feeling on the yoke and throttle is still awkward. And the angle of view of runway centerline over the nose is... well, different.

When I pull into the parking area, I find an empty ramp. During recent visits, this airport has been low in activity, but never have I been the only airplane on the ramp. Of course, there are aircraft in the hangars, but still this is disturbing. The depressed aviation environment since 2008 is in full effect, and nowhere is it more noticeable than at small general aviation airports. It's nice to have the place to myself, but not a good sign for the industry.

Empty parking ramp at Siletz Bay Airport, Oregon

After putting up my tent, I decide to walk to the golf course lodge, where I should find an Internet connection and a fancy restaurant. I'm not in the mood for fancy, but it's a nice menu, although quite pricey. Usually, I eat at the Side Door Cafe, right across Highway 101, but tonight I want to use the Internet, and the walk will do me good. It's a pleasant, cool evening, with still enough sunlight to keep me visible to vehicles on the highway as I walk. After dinner, I can get a ride from the lodge or take the parallel road on the other side of Highway 101, which is a safer trek at night.

As I walk to the lodge, the shoulders of the highway are wide and seemingly safe. But there are lots of fast semi-trailers on the road, so it's not a comfortable stroll. When I reach the golf course, I slip off the side of the road and follow the golf cart path up to the lodge. It's a good shortcut and a route less hectic.

I'm dressed in shorts and a T-shirt, appropriate for the season, but maybe not for the main restaurant. The suited man who greets me at the door gives me a suspicious look.

"Can I eat dressed like this?" I ask.

"We can find you a seat, sir," he replies.

As soon as I enter the dining room, I can see I'm the only customer. I guess my lack of suit and tie is acceptable during a recession. After all, I've brought my wallet.

I take my assigned seat and plop my backpack on the chair next to me. The suited host picks it up and moves it out of sight below the table.

"Let's put this down here," he says.

That's good, because I wouldn't want to embarrass any of the other patrons, if they eventually arrive.

"Maybe you should remove your hat," he says.

"Sure, I can do that," I say.

I forgot – I'm not in Canada anymore.

But I'm not embarrassed, nor am I offended by the host's words. He seems almost apologetic, and I'm sure he doesn't want to scare off the only business tonight.

When the waitress arrives, I'm immediately at ease. She appreciates my company in the empty restaurant. When she hears I've walked from the airport, she insists on contacting the lodge desk and arranging transportation back. But I tell her I'd rather walk, and she finally accepts graciously.

"Watch out on the highway. It's getting awfully dark," she says.

"I'll cross over and walk along the parallel road. It's an easy walk."

"Oh," she replies, with a look of surprise. "I didn't know there was a road over there."

Sometimes, when traveling by small airplane, you get to explore routes even locals don't seem to know. When you're dependent on your feet for transportation, you get a good sense of the local geography.

After dinner, I use the Internet connection in the lobby to update myself on an important (to me) college football game. I check my email and the weather forecast for tomorrow. Then I file an IFR flight plan, and walk upstairs to see what the pub looks like. A pizza and ribs menu is posted on the door that looks appetizing for future visits, and it looks like it's shorts and T-shirt friendly.

After crossing the highway, I walk along the road between the main highway and the beach. The shoulders are wide for walking, and I encounter few cars (and no trucks). I turn right onto Laurel Road, which takes me past trailers and small houses, directly to the beach. At the end of the road, a wide sand path opens onto the broad beach with its pounding surf. This is my favorite place to access the beach, less than a mile south of the airport. A closer location is Stevens Road, which leads to a dead end where you get a good view of the shore, but a cliff blocks entry to the beach. In this part of Glen Eden Beach, modern mansions lining the seashore contrast with inexpensive modular homes only a few hundred feet inland.

I continue north along the parallel road again, past the tavern and to the tiny post office adjacent to the Side Door Cafe. This is one of my favorite restaurants, easily accessible by walking out the airport access road and directly across the highway. A series of dilapidated wooden steps lead up to the restaurant. The word "cafe" is a bit informal for this fine and somewhat pricey restaurant, but you can easily make a meal out of their tasty appetizers.

When I get back to the airport, I stop at the entrance to the parking ramp. It's quite dark now, even with a bright first-quarter moon providing plenty of light for an evening walk. My tent sits next to the Arrow, on the far end of the empty ramp. I can hear the crashing surf from my camping spot. No wonder Siletz Bay is one of my all time favorites.

* * * * *

THE REST OF THE TRIP SOUTH to Los Angeles goes nearly flawlessly. The airport at North Bend has a new name since my last visit – Southwest Regional Airport. At first, I figure my chart is in error, since this is the Pacific Northwest, not the Southwest, but then I realize the airport is named based on its position in Oregon near the southwest corner. More surprising is the presence of a new control tower at this previously uncontrolled airport, a fact I almost missed when I first checked the Brown Book. The control tower is so new on my day of arrival that it's considered an "advisory tower," practicing for the official opening.

I'm sure today's NOTAMs carried this information, but the ATIS broadcast bails me out of potential embarrassment when trying to understand the strange ATC language being used today: "Tower advises no reported traffic." Or, worse yet, landing while tuned into the old Unicom frequency rather than the new control tower.

If you've ever tried to conscientiously check NOTAMs during an Internet self-briefing (which is a perfectly legal briefing, and certainly safe), you'll appreciate my back-to-back lack of NOTAM data for Ocean Shores and North Bend's advisory control tower. The number of NOTAMs nationwide on any particular day is overwhelming. FSS telephone briefers work with the system all the time and make it seem easy during direct-phone briefings. Still, self-briefings are more common for all of us these days.

On the ground at Southwest Regional (which most pilots will forever call North Bend), I'm met by two sets of parking marshallers who wanted my gas business. Gas wars! – just like the good ol' days – a product of the struggling aviation economy trying to grow at a rejuvenated airport.

The new airline terminal at Southwest Regional is nearly empty, with no airplanes at the gates. But the modern building boasts three levels in attractive metal-and-glass architecture, with a tiny cafe and a waitress who seems surprised to find me there for breakfast.

"Just moved in," she says. "This used to be a big closet."

Someday soon, this will be a busy airline terminal, complete with an active (not advisory) control tower. Or so someone thinks.

After my leisurely breakfast, I return to my aircraft, and taxi the lengthy route to the end of the runway. I've learned to avoid intersection takeoffs, even on long runways. As the old saying goes: "You can't use pavement that's behind you."

Climbing out of North Bend under clear skies, I continue southbound on Victor 27, refueling at Monterey, south of San Francisco. Then I press on down the airway towards Oceano Airport, near San Luis Obispo. This is another of my favorite airport campgrounds, right on the beach, like Siletz Bay. But even under the clear skies that surround me 20 miles north of Oceano, I can see low clouds lining the coast farther south. After cancelling flight following with Los Angeles Center, I begin my descent to the airport, still about 10 miles north. I'm heading towards the line marking the edge of the coastal clouds, about a mile inland. My GPS indicates the airport is right at the edge of the low stratus, meaning there's a 50-50 chance the airport itself will be in the clear.

By the time I pass over the GPS position for the airport at 2000 feet, it's obvious the airport is beneath the clouds. There's no runway to see, although it's clear less than a mile to the east. This stratus layer typically stretches almost to the surface, making flight under the clouds impossible. Without an instrument approach, Oceano is perched on the edge of weather minimums. Today there's no hope.

So, after a flight I was determined to complete as a slow three-day trek south along the coast, I pop back up into Los Angeles Center's airspace on the second day, and request flight following to Cable Airport, inland from Los Angeles. My original plan was to try out two or three airport camping locations along the way, and I only ended up spending one night – at my favorite airport, Siletz Bay. But the flight has been relaxing and enjoyable, except for my awkwardness in the left seat.

By the time I land at Cable Airport, I'm still struggling with my left hand on the yoke and right hand on the throttle. It may be the last time I'm ever tempted to fly from the left seat, solo or otherwise. I'll take the familiar right seat any day, thank you.

◊ ◊ ◊ ◊ ◊ ◊

Chapter 13

Renewal

Burlington-Skagit Regional and Port Angeles WA

FOR SEVERAL YEARS after relocating my Arrow from Powell River, British Columbia, to Bellingham, Washington, the airplane experienced minimum activity. Margy and I flew less than 50 hours annually, our flight time deteriorating to the point where it was mostly inactivity flights around the traffic pattern at Bellingham or local hops to the nearby islands.

As my biennial flight review approached in 2013, I prepared once again for the arrival of David from Los Angeles. As I always tell my aviation friends: "It's hard to find a good flight instructor in Washington, so I import mine from California."

Which is, of course, a lie, at least partially. It's true David is a great flight instructor and a fellow I always enjoy flying with under any circumstances. But the rest of the story is that I really don't know any flight instructors in Washington, and I'm simply comfortable with David. Every other spring, it gives us an excuse to get together for a long weekend of intense flying, David coming north on Alaska Airlines to join me for a fun-filled weekend of Bellingham Slam basketball, boating, and lots of flying in the Arrow. This year we add a WNBA basketball game in Seattle and our first real experience with RNAV instrument approaches.

Both David and I know enough about RNAV to talk a good story. Area Navigation is a set of IFR procedures that includes GPS approaches. When I finished up my aeronautics teaching career at Mount San Antonio College in 2005, GPS approaches were already becoming the norm, and I knew enough to teach them to my students.

But I really hadn't flown any RNAV approaches, and that situation continued even after my Arrow was upgraded to a WAAS version of the Garmin 430 GPS several years ago and became fully certified for RNAV approaches.

Now with David's arrival approaching, I've allowed the RNAV certification of the Garmin GPS to expire, and I've flown IFR less and less, including traditional VOR-ILS navigation. Meanwhile, RNAV approaches have mushroomed nationwide, with Bellingham now possessing precision LPV GPS approaches from both ends of Runway 16/34. Additionally, most of our local airports have adopted RNAV approaches, many of them LPV (Localizer Performance with Vertical Guidance), with glide path and weather minimums equal to the traditional Instrument Landing System. Meanwhile, in recent months, the Arrow has flown mostly around the traffic pattern at Bellingham, seldom venturing into the IFR system, and still without attempting a single RNAV approach. This was about to change dramatically.

"Don't check the tach very closely," I say to John, the local maintenance shop chief who performs my annual inspections at Bellingham.

"Oh, no," he replies. "Not another year like last one, I hope."

"Worse, I'm afraid."

"How much worse," he accuses with raised eyebrows.

"Seven hours," is my muted reply. Maybe he'll think I said 'seventy.'

"Seven! Wayne, you've got to find an excuse to fly."

"I'd prefer a reason rather than an excuse."

"Well, you need either a reason or an excuse," he replies. "I've got a customer who slipped badly in his flying hours last year," responds John. "So he bought an old house on the beach down in Oregon. Now he flies there all the time, which puts lots of hours on his airplane."

"Sounds expensive. I sure don't need an old house."

"Well, you need something!" says John. "Come up with some rationale to get back in the air."

Of course, John's business depends on customers who have purposes to fly, no matter how feeble their reasons or excuses may be. In my case, I shouldn't need an excuse. Margy and I have spent a good portion of our life together traveling around the country in small airplanes, enjoying every flight, and developing plenty of reasons to get into the air. But not in recent years. It's time this situation changed.

* * * * *

I'VE ALWAYS ENJOYED FLYING IFR. In fact, I'm more at home in an instrument cross-country environment than operating VFR. Part of the reason involves the enjoyment Margy and I experience flying together. Under IFR, there's plenty for both of us to do, and we thrive on the teamwork. Add the new challenge of RNAV approaches to the mix, and IFR will be even more exciting. We love seeking out remote airports that allow camping next to our airplane, and that's all the motivation we need to get back into flying. The RNAV portion of the equation should assist with the process of IFR renewal. But first both the pilots and their avionics panel need attention.

I download the latest Garmin 430W simulator, and begin playing with RNAV approaches. Additionally, I purchase a traditional (VOR-ILS) IFR flight simulator for my laptop (X-Plane), including a yoke and throttle quadrant, and begin flying the local airspace in my living room. After years of flying out of Bellingham, I'm experienced with the local departure procedures. Now I'm getting reacquainted with the Kieno Four Departure and comfortable with the Bellingham ILS and RNAV approaches, at least in simulation. It feels wonderful, and just in time for David's arrival from California.

I update the built-in electronic IFR charts in the Garmin 430W, and establish an appointment at Burlington-Skagit Airport for an overhaul of the airplane's avionics. The number-two NavCom (an old KX170B) is adequate as the second radio, but the communication receiver is weak, and the VOR-ILS is completely inoperative. My ancient King DME is also inop, and the backup Northstar GPS-LORAN is no longer supported for navigation upgrades (plus the LORAN equipment is just extra weight along for the ride, since the ground stations were decommissioned nationwide in 2010). The Arrow's avionics need a makeover, and there's no time like the present. If this is going to be a renewal, we might as well dive into it big-time.

Avionics renovations, of course, don't come cheap. Nor do they typically stay on schedule. In the case of the trip to avionics shop at

Burlington-Skagit Airport, the output date slips further as the shop technician finds old wiring untouched in nearly forty years.

"Some of the wires just dead-end," says Bob over the phone. "Many of the connections are old and corroded. Just touch them, and they fall apart."

In other words, it gets a lot worse before it gets better. When I visit the Skagit hangar halfway through the renovation, I gasp at the sight of my lovable Arrow's cockpit stripped down, with gaping holes where the instruments and radios used to be. It's hard to imagine how the avionics equipment will ever work in harmony again.

Instrument panel avionics overhaul, Skagit Regional Airport

The output date is pushing up against David's arrival. When it slips again to just a few days before his inbound flight on Alaska Airlines, I imagine a weekend of flying simulators to accomplish my flight review. But then everything seems to fall into place, and the Arrow is ready for pickup.

On the first flight, during my trip back to Bellingham, I set the Garmin 430W up for the RNAV approach into Runway 34. While tracking inbound along the LPV track in VFR, I'm so overwhelmed with the beauty of what's happening that I make my first call to Bellingham Tower right at the edge of the Class D airspace. The tower offers no criticism, but I'm embarrassed to find myself so far behind the airplane. Obviously, learning RNAV approaches will require care and attention to the details of what's happening outside the cockpit as well as inside.

* * * * *

WHEN DAVID ARRIVES ON FRIDAY, we spend our first evening together discussing Bellingham's traditional ILS approach as well as local RNAV procedures. David is quick to admit his experience with GPS approaches has been primarily in the classroom, just like me, so this will be a steep learning curve for both of us. We pull out the local IFR charts and discuss the area's RNAV approaches, trying to agree on details neither of us fully understand.

"You know what they always say," I note to David. "There's nothing more dangerous in the cockpit than two flight instructors, except maybe two instrument flight instructors."

Did I mention that both David and I are instrument flight instructors?

"I'd call it the blind leading the blind," replied David. "Since ATC is getting used to these new approaches, too, that makes three of us."

We laugh it off, as we always do. There's nothing like hangar-flying with David to put me in a good mood.

After fussing over the charts, and raising more questions than answers, we fly the ILS approach in the X-Plane simulator, and then turn to the 430W computer trainer. Before we know it, it's after midnight. It's time to get some sleep in preparation for our first flight in the morning.

* * * * *

I STAY UP EVEN LATER THAN DAVID, trying to file IFR flight plans for the next day. Since it's been a few months since I've filed IFR, I'm greeted with a new requirement. All departing IFR flight plans from Bellingham now require an ICAO flight plan. Departures from other destinations can still use my previously stored DUATS IFR flight plans (even flights to Bellingham), but Bellingham is now on the list of airports requiring ICAO flight plans for departure. That's obviously related to our nearness to the Canadian border – the first IFR departure control facility, even going southbound, is Victoria Terminal. Bellingham sits within Canadian airspace.

I've intended to learn the intricacies of the ICAO format, but not particularly in the middle of the night. I struggle for a few hours, and finally file my first flight plan for our morning departure from Bellingham to Arlington. With one ICAO flight plan complete, each of the next is simple by comparison. Before I go to bed, N41997 has a round-trip IFR route established to Arlington and return. After that, we'll head south to Anacortes and destinations still undetermined for the rest of the day.

My IFR renewal has obviously begun, and I haven't even left my living room.

*****

THE NEXT MORNING, I preflight the Arrow outside the hangar, while David looks over the local IFR en route low altitude chart. He has been in contact with Brandon, who now works at Bellingham Airport, a "young kid" we both know from California, where he used to work at the local airport, Brackett Field. Brandon saw me one day at Bellingham (more correctly, he saw my maroon-and-white Arrow in the open hangar), and came over to say hello. What a pleasant surprise to see him in Port of Bellingham coveralls. In California, he would routinely show up at my Arrow's parking spot with the airport fuel truck, cheerfully ready to top off my tanks, and now he's working at Bellingham. On the day I saw him, he was driving a Port of Bellingham pickup truck, and I assumed he was doing similar airport duties as in California. We only had a few minutes to chat before he got a call on his radio and had to depart, but I passed his email address on to David.

"Brandon says he's working today," notes David as I stoop under the right wing to check the landing gear strut, brake, and wheel well. "He says he'll try to stop by with his truck."

It seems like a strange statement, but I simply mutter: "Uh-huh." I assume Brandon has a new truck he's proud of, or maybe he means the airport pickup.

Just as I crawl out from under the wing, I see bright, flashing lights headed straight at us from the taxiway, a huge fire truck. Suddenly,

Brandon and David at Bellingham Airport, Washington

I get it. Brandon has come a long way since refueling my Arrow in California.

A few minutes later, we're airborne on the Kieno Four Departure to Arlington. We begin our IFR review with the localizer approach to Runway 34, followed by a missed approach, and then pick up our IFR flight plan on file for Bellingham.

We request the GPS LPV approach to Runway 16 at Bellingham, thus executing our first IFR RNAV approach, letting George, the autopilot, intercept the course and engage the vertical glide path. It's a flawless trip inbound, as we watch George execute a precise descent to decision height.

"It's not just the blind leading the blind," I say to David, once we're climbing out on the assigned missed approach. "It's George leading the blind."

"Two instrument flight instructors fumbling with RNAV approaches for the first time," says David over the intercom. "And air traffic controllers at Victoria Terminal controlling an aircraft in the

U.S. There's a lot of learning going on today, but I'm not sure who's in charge."

"You know who's in charge – George, of course," I reply. "He's going to teach us RNAV approaches, despite ourselves."

David laughs, and then composes himself as he punches the mike button to cancel our IFR flight plan and request VFR flight following for our departure for Anacortes to the south.

* * * * *

AFTER A BRIEF BREAK on the ground at Anacortes Airport, we "pop-up" with Whidbey Approach Control for the RNAV approach at Friday Harbor. We walk downtown for lunch, and then we're airborne again, back to Bellingham for the ILS.

David at Friday Harbor, San Juan Islands

* * * * *

THE NEXT MORNING, we fly IFR to Port Angeles for the RNAV approach to Runway 27, followed by a missed approach and some holding pattern practice, where I fumble enough to cause some self-criticism.

"What was that?" I comment to David. "I tried a parallel entry, which turned into a modified teardrop, followed by a tracking maneuver inbound that I've never seen in the textbook."

""Well, you tried," answers David with a smile. "You know what they say – any holding pattern entry that keeps you within 5 miles of the fix is a good one."

"ATC doesn't really care, do they? As long as we don't bust their template for protected airspace."

"No, they never pay much attention to holds," says David. "I think they realize most pilots are just floundering through assigned holding patterns anyway. But I think our problem is that we had the nav needle pointed outbound when we should have selected the inbound course. The blind leading the blind again."

"Even George looks lost," I reply.

After our holding pattern fiasco (which is one of the primary reasons instrument practice in good weather conditions is so important), we execute Port Angeles' ILS Runway 9 approach before returning home to Bellingham for another ILS. It's two days of intense instrument training, interspersed with basketball and more basketball – ideal medicine for my personal airborne renewal.

* * * * *

IN THE WEEKS FOLLOWING DAVID'S VISIT, Margy and I launch on a series of IFR flights, usually ending with a practice RNAV approach that finds us camped next to our Arrow at some of the Pacific Northwest's most beautiful airports. Now that I'm trained in RNAV (at least basically), I pass my accumulated knowledge on to Margy. We fly with renewed self-confidence, and we're at a peak of enjoyment regarding the wonders of flight. I'm determined never to allow my flying skills to deteriorate again from self-imposed neglect. And it clearly shows each time the engine of N41997 roars to life once again.

Chapter 14

Why Favorites are Favorites
Siletz Bay Or and Chehalis WA

I'M BACK IN THE SADDLE AGAIN, navigating through the IFR environment comfortably, and it feels great. The mental attention demanded by flying an airplane is unsurpassed by any other process in life. The skills and mindset required of the human brain are totally satisfying.

As soon as Margy and I settle into our new determination to go airborne frequently, we tackle a round-trip that's reminiscent of many trips in the past. In fact, that's exactly why we choose it to begin the process of IFR self-renewal. When you establish favorites, whether it is airports, sports teams, hiking trails, or anything else in life, you don't need to justify why you keep returning to the same choices over and over again. You return because it's enjoyable. For Margy and I, just the thought of leaving for one of our favorite destinations is enough to brighten our dispositions. So it is with favorite airport camping spots.

On a warm afternoon in early July, Margy and I depart from Bellingham's Runway 16, the Arrow requiring less pavement than expected for a departure on a hot day at maximum gross weight. The rear seat is full of personal baggage, an ice chest, and a variety of charts, books, and aviation supplies. In the baggage compartment, our camping gear fills the area nearly to the roof, although its mostly lighter objects, including a tent, air mattress, sleeping bags, and folding chairs.

We've fueled the Arrow to the tabs at Bellingham, rather than full tanks, to keep the weight down. Our destination is one of our favorites (again), Siletz Bay on the Oregon coast, and our fuel load will be adequate under almost any conditions concerning the winds aloft. Our to-the-tabs gas departing Bellingham will help the Arrow get airborne on Siletz's 3300-foot runway the next morning. We haven't flown with our full camping load in some time, so it's best to make sure we're reacquainted with the airplane's performance under controlled conditions.

Our plan is to fly farther south from Siletz Bay the next morning, to the closest airport with fuel, Newport, Oregon, another favorite. Then we'll retrace our route home with a second night's stop at Chehalis, Washington. A favorite (Siletz Bay) followed by another favorite (Newport) followed by another favorite (Chehalis). When you pilot your own aircraft, you get to decide where you go, so why not take advantage of it?

The plan works fine, although we obviously could have handled topped-off fuel tanks departing Bellingham, as evidenced by the shorter-than-expected pavement used during our takeoff at Siletz Bay the next day. Still, it's always good to be light when departing a relatively short runway.

The IFR flight south to Siletz Bay is smooth the entire way. Margy notes how the oil pressure gauge rides one-needle-width into the green arc during cruise, right where she expects it to be. And I notice the CGT and EGT on all four cylinders are running at the precise values I've become accustomed to seeing. One thing nice about being familiar with an airplane is how comfortable it is to see instrument values that make you feel at home, fostering a relaxed flight environment.

Headwinds from the south throughout our flight to Siletz Bay drop our GPS groundspeed to a rather consistent 110 knots, twenty knots below our no-wind velocity, but we have a good buffer of fuel. We land at Siletz Bay with about 6 gallons usable fuel in each tank, which is nearly an hour's reserve beyond what will be needed for the short flight to Newport the next morning. Still, when you see fuel gauges in an airplane drop to the one-quarter mark, it's time to pay attention.

Final approach at Siletz Bay

Siletz Bay is just as we always seem to find it – a choppy approach on final when landing to the north and a nearly empty ramp, perfect conditions for camping.

We park at the rear of the nearly empty parking area, pushing the Arrow back to the edge of the pavement. I walk the short path into the trees to retrieve the wooden picnic table bench that's sat there for a number of years. With our tent in the grass behind our airplane, we'll prop our feet up on the bench in front of our folding chairs. Familiarity brings peaceful contentment.

That evening, we cross the highway (the most dangerous part of the trip) to climb the old wooden steps leading up to the Back Door Cafe. The stairs are encroached by berry bushes to the extent you wouldn't even notice the path unless you were looking for it.

After dinner, back at our campsite, we sit in the developing shadows of the setting sun, the air turning quickly cooler. Before it's totally dark, we crawl into our tent, and are soon sound asleep.

Siletz Bay camping area

* * * * *

DURING THE TIME I'VE BEEN AWAY from serious IFR in the Arrow, the aviation environment has changed. To me, the greatest improvements are RNAV approaches and the advent of a national system for providing IFR clearances by telephone. Dial the phone number, and you're ready to pick up your clearance from any location with cell phone coverage. In the case of Siletz Bay, you can go airborne with an IFR clearance already in hand. Previously, it was often necessary to climb in scud-running fashion through the early morning coastal stratus to clear conditions on-top, where an IFR clearance could be obtained through Seattle Center. Cell phone clearances in the run-up area are a vast improvement and a convenience, as well as an important advancement in safety.

On the phone in the run-up area, I copy my IFR clearance to Newport, and receive a generous clearance void time. We're airborne and climbing through the low broken stratus layer a few minutes later. Seattle Center, however, is busy with traffic, and it's tough to get a word in edgewise. Finally it's "radar contact," and Seattle is vectoring us towards the ILS approach course at Newport.

Considering our fuel situation, ATC's radar vectors are extended longer than I'd prefer. Besides the congestion on frequency, there are other indications the local airspace is nearly saturated: "Niner-Niner-Seven, this vector will take you across the localizer for spacing."

The expected fifteen-minute flight takes over a half hour, reducing our fuel margin if we need to make a missed approach with subsequent diversion to an alternate inland airport that sits in the sunshine.

Finally cleared for the Runway 16 ILS, I fly a sloppy approach most of the way down, with the localizer and glideslope needles looking like they are in a sword fight, swinging in every direction. Maybe it's my preoccupation with our fuel status. We break out 500 feet above ground, with the runway straight in front of us.

Once we're down, I pull into an open parking spot, but keep the engine running while I try to close our IFR flight plan with Seattle Center. I can hear ATC only intermittently, and they can't hear me at all, so I finally switch to the FSS frequency, and get immediate assistance with closing the flight plan.

Besides the dreaded self-serve pumps, Newport now sports a fuel truck, which meets us at our parking spot. Margy and I make a bet regarding how much fuel will be required to fill the tanks. As usual, I guess low, and she guesses high, which is a good indication of our personalities. We've both been concerned with our minimal fuel reserve, with Margy showing more cautious concern than me. The pump stops at 41 gallons, which means we landed with 9 gallons remaining. This equates to 7 usable gallons.

"We only had 40 minutes of fuel left, not an acceptable margin," I say. "As usual, you were right about cutting it way too close."

As we departed Siletz Bay, Margy had expressed hesitation about this flight, noting we didn't know how much maneuvering ATC would require to set us up for the approach. (She was right – it was more than expected.)

"And I don't like the weather situation," she added. "If we have to go inland to find an alternate, we're at bare minimums."

The latest METAR before departing Siletz Bay showed Newport with a 300-foot overcast and a mile and a half visibility, barely above ILS minimums, as verified by my cell phone call to FSS. But there were extenuating circumstances (as there nearly always are), including my desire to fly an ILS approach nearly down to minimums in actual instrument conditions. Sometimes desires masquerade as reasons, when in fact they're often merely rationalizations. As usual, Margy was right, and I'm quick to admit it.

"We could have waited before departing Siletz Bay," I note as we watch the Newport fuel attendant wind up his hose. "Conditions were improving all along the coast this morning, and we could have jumped over here VFR quickly by waiting a little longer, saving at least 15 minutes of gas and eliminating the what-if challenge of an IFR missed approach and flight to an alternate. It would have made a big difference."

Margy doesn't gloat over it. She's right, and we both know it. I'm wrong, but I've learned from it. Live and learn, but make sure you keep living. Getting recurrent in flying involves more than physical and mental skills. It involves attitude shifts every step of the way.

At Newport, we find the fixed-base operator under different management, but still excelling in its dedicated attention to arriving pilots. We walk over to the open hangar, where a black Crown Victoria sits next to a turboprop Pilatus. This place is still very much the same, with old and new side-by-side.

From Newport, we travel northbound on Victor 27. Seattle Center's frequency is rather quiet now, so I take the opportunity to ask the controller a question about one of the RNAV approaches into Astoria, an instrument procedure I fumbled with just a few days ago. I'm not sure how to transition to this approach from our current direction of flight, and the controller is pleased to talk me through it. While he explains the intricacies of the approach, I smile at his enthusiasm to share what he knows. It's an example of the love of the aviation environment shared by pilots and controllers alike.

My flight plans these days carry the remarks "IFR Training Flight," which is my way of telling each controller along the way that Margy and I are practicing IFR and learning all the time, and that we want more. On numerous occasions, I've noticed ATC sending us to fixes where holding pattern course reversals and more elaborate procedures are required. This seems to be their acknowledgement of our desire to experience all aspects of the environment during IFR training, which is certainly fine with us. It also proves that remarks added to a flight plan are actually forwarded to ATC and read by them, which encourages me to use "Remarks" whenever I see fit.

Over Astoria, we continue north direct to RELTE waypoint for the RNAV Runway 16 approach into Chehalis. This takes us well beyond the airport, so we look down on the runway in clear conditions as we pass overhead. Some would say this is a waste of flying time (and fuel) under visual meteorological conditions. I say it's a great way to get comfortable with GPS approaches. In this case, we're cleared for the holding pattern course reversal at RELTE, which takes us within a mile of Olympia Airport (but protected by IFR separation standards), and then back south to Chehalis.

Since other aircraft at Chehalis are using Runway 34, we swing off the Runway 16 final approach course to circle to land. A glider reports that he is inbound a few miles west of the airport, noting he's still "a long ways out," and there will be plenty of time for us to land in front of him. I'm never comfortable with gliders in the pattern, so I make a short approach, flying a tight base leg. After landing, I exit the runway as soon as speed permits, giving the glider plenty of room to land.

"Nobody in the camping area," says Margy, as I pull onto the parallel taxiway.

We've never been here when someone else is camping, even though the camping area is one of our favorites. Some would call this spot too busy for comfortable camping, since it's next to the self-serve fuel island. But its fun to watch airplanes come and go at the pumps. On a hot day like today, we can set our tent under the cool of the big maple tree. Pilots and airport personnel pass by frequently, always with a friendly wave.

"No one has offered us a ride yet," says Margy, as we set up our tent.

I laugh at her remark, remembering one of the notable things about this fine airport. Usually, on any visit to the camping area, several people stop by to ask if we need a ride. A very friendly place.

With the golf course's rooftop dining area right across the street, there's no need to ride anywhere, but the offers of hospitality are always appreciated. We enjoy walking to the nearby shopping center, too, so what more could we want? And this is a campsite with a perfect view of the gas pumps! For pilots, these are the kind of things that explains why favorites are favorites.

Chehalis camping area

About the Author

From 1980 to 2005, Wayne Lutz was Chairman of the Aeronautics Department at Mount San Antonio College in Los Angeles. He also served 20 years as a U.S. Air Force C-130 aircraft maintenance officer. His educational background includes a B.S. degree in physics from the University of Buffalo and an M.S. in systems management from the University of Southern California. The author is a flight instructor with 7000 hours of flying experience.

For three decades, he spent summers in Canada, exploring remote regions in his Piper Arrow and camping next to his airplane. The author resides in a floating cabin on Canada's Powell Lake in all seasons, and occasionally in a city-folk condo in Bellingham, Washington. His writing genres include regional Canadian publications and science fiction.

Books by Wayne J. Lutz

Coastal British Columbia Stories

Up the Lake
Up the Main
Up the Winter Trail
Up the Strait
Up the Airway
Farther Up the Lake
Farther Up the Main
Farther Up the Strait
Cabin Number 5
Off the Grid
Up the Inlet

Pacific Northwest Titles

Flying the Pacific Northwest
Paddling the Pacific Northwest

Science Fiction Titles

Echo of a Distant Planet
Inbound to Earth
Anomaly at Fortune Lake
When Galaxies Collide
Across the Galactic Sea

Order at: www.PowellRiverBooks.com

Appendix A
Cockpit Instruments and Avionics

N41997 cockpit -- 1974 Piper Arrow II

ADF (top) and Northstar GPS-LORAN (bottom)

DME (top-right); VOR (bottom-right) shows slightly off-course; Flight Director with annunciator panel (below DME) and command bars (top left); HSI (bottom-left) shows on-course indication

Throttle quadrant: throttle (left-black); prop control (center-blue); mixture control (right-red). CHT-EGT gauge at right.

Horizontal Situation Indicator (HSI) during Instrument Landing System (ILS) approach. Aircraft is intercepting the course from the left, and nearly on glide slope ("bugs" to left and right side)

Garmin GPS (GNS 430) with audio panel (above)

CHT/EGT gauge: currently monitoring cylinder #1 for cylinder head temperature and exhaust gas temperature

Pilot's yoke: autopilot disconnect button (right); electric pitch trim (split switch); CWS (control wheel steering to override autopilot)

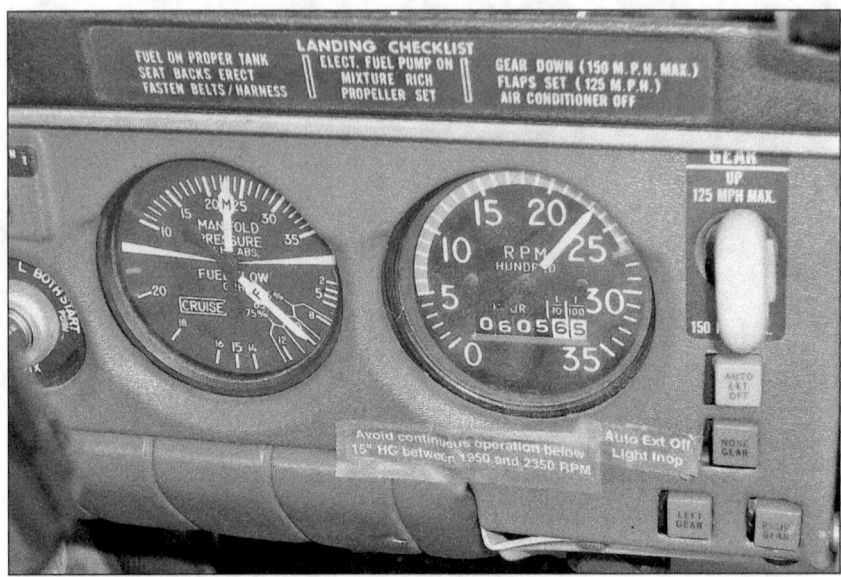

Manifold pressure (top-left, controlled by throttle); fuel flow (bottom-left, controlled by mixture lever); RPM (right, controlled by prop lever); landing gear down-and-locked lights (green) below gear extension handle

Transponder with standard VFR squawk (beacon) code of 1200

Appendix B
Aviation Terminology and Acronyms

Automated Weather Observing System (AWOS) – Automated weather reports updated every few minutes and broadcast on a designated frequency at uncontrolled airports..

Air Route Traffic Control Center or "Center" (ARTCC) – ATC facilities that cover airspace above and between Approach Control facilities.

Air Traffic Control (ATC) – Nav Canada controllers or Federal Aviation Administration (FAA) specialists in the U.S.

Approach Control – ATC facility, usually radar equipped, for assisting pilots during approach and departure; called "Terminal Control" in Canada.

Area Navigation (RNAV) – IFR point-to-point navigation to waypoints, including instrument approaches. GPS is the most common RNAV system.

Automated Terminal Information System (ATIS) – recorded airport information, available on a discrete frequency prior to arrival and departure at most airports with an active control tower.

Automatic Direction Finder (ADF) – navigational indicator that allows tracking to-from non-directional beacons (NDBs).

Class B Airspace – airspace surrounding the nation's busiest airports, such as Seattle, where all flights are radar controlled by Approach Control.

Class C Airspace – airspace surrounding major airports, such as Whidbey Naval Air Station where all traffic is monitored by Approach Control. Communication is required by all aircraft operating within this airspace.

Class D Airspace – airspace surrounding less-busy airports with operating control towers, such as Bellingham. Communication with the control tower is required within this airspace.

Cylinder Head Temperature (CHT) – a direct indication of engine overheat condition; particularly important during climb.

Density Altitude – mathematical computation of the thickness of the air, as perceived by an airfoil, due to temperature, pressure, humidity, and actual altitude; e.g. density altitude may be 5000 feet at a sea level airport on a hot, humid, low pressure day.

Direct User Access Terminal Service (DUATS) – FAA contracted services for pilot self-briefing via personal computer. Provides pilots with weather data and the capability to submit IFR and VFR flight plans directly to ATC.

Distance Measuring Equipment (DME) – provides digital reading of distance to a VOR or other ground station; not as accurate as GPS distance due to slant range error that increases with altitude.

Empennage – the tail section of an airplane, including the elevator, rudder, and horizontal and vertical stabilizer. In the case of a Piper Arrow, this includes the stabilator and anti-servo tab.

Exhaust Gas Temperature (EGT) – temperature that provides an indication of proper mixture control; high EGT indicates a mixture that is too lean.

Federal Aviation Regulations (FARs) – Recreational flights generally operate under FAR Part 91, both VFR and IFR.

Flight Director (FD) – sophisticated avionics, usually limited to large aircraft, that provide the pilot with additional navigational and attitude data; usually used in conjunction with an autopilot.

Flight Plan – FAA filed information for a VFR or IFR flight. Pilots provide information in accordance with a specific list of data proposed for a specific flight.

Flight Service Station (FSS) – FAA facility that provides preflight weather briefings and in-flight information to pilots; this service is not ATC, but can relay information to ATC.

Fuel Flow Gauge – used for initial leaning of the fuel-air mixture, in conjunction with EGT gauge; indicator calibrated in gallons/hour.

Global Positioning System (GPS) – alternate navigation system, replacing common VOR airways and instrument approaches; not all aviation GPS units are certified for IFR.

Instrument Flight Rules (IFR) – operation in accordance with standards that allow flight in almost any weather conditions; requires special pilot certification, equipment, and flight planning procedures.

Instrument Landing System (ILS) – a precision approach system with vertical glide slope, available at major airports. IFR aircraft can land using an ILS when cloud heights are as low as 200 feet and during minimal visibilities (typically less than 1/2 mile).

Localizer Approach (LOC) – a non-precision approach system similar to the ILS, but with no glide slope and higher weather minimums.

Localizer Performance with Vertical Guidance (LPV) – RNAV instrument approach that allows descent to a decision height similar to the precision of the ILS approach, including vertical glide path navigation.

Long Range Navigation (LORAN) – an older area navigation system adopted from marine use. LORAN-C, the current format, has generally been replaced by GPS, and is projected for decommissioning by 2010.

Manifold Pressure (MP) – an indicator of engine power, measured in inches of Mercury; this gauge is provided on engines with constant-speed propellers; increased throttle position provides increased manifold pressure.

Mixture Control – cockpit lever that allows adjustment of the fuel-air mixture; engines are leaned for operation at higher altitudes.

Mode-C – cockpit transponder function that provides altitude readout information to air traffic control radar facilities

Multicom – common frequency used at airports without any established frequency (122.9 MHz); multicom also refers to an air-to-air frequency between aircraft that is selected by the pilots.

Non-directional Beacon (NDB) – navigational beacons used for instrument approaches. ADF receivers and indicators are used for NDB navigation.

NOTAM – Notice to Airmen; changes to airports or navaids, including new obstacles and information not yet printed on charts. NOTAMS should be checked prior to flight, readily available from FSS.

Prop Control – cockpit lever for adjusting the blade angle of a constant-speed propeller; push forward for less pitch and higher RPM.

Squawk (or Squawk Code) - four-digit code set into a transponder that provides ATC with aircraft identification and altitude.

Terminal (Terminal Control) – Canadian ATC facility, usually radar-equipped, that handles aircraft in approach and departure phases of flight or for low-alitude passage through an area.

Transponder – radar beacon transmitter in an aircraft that provides continuous data to ATC, including position information: mode-C transponders provide additional altitude information.

Unicom – a non-ATC radio communication station at small airports that provides non-regulatory information such as wind and advisories regarding known traffic.

VHF Omnidirectional Range (VOR) – common equipment for enroute navigation and many non-precision instrument approaches; this system is gradually being replaced by GPS navigation.

Victor Airway (e.g., V27) – established routes between VORs used by most IFR traffic and many VFR aircraft.

Visual Flight Rules (VFR) – flight by reference to the ground in weather conditions with good visibilities and few clouds.

Waypoint – an electronic checkpoint location used in GPS navigation; sometimes called "phantom stations" since they are not dependent upon the location of VORs and NDBs.

Appendix C
Airport Index

Anacortes WA   p.17, 20, 23-26, 136, 138
Arlington WA   p.38-40, 77, 111-113, 117-118, 136-137, 141-143
Astoria OR   p.63, 94, 125, 145-146
Bella Bella WA   p.60
Bellingham WA   p.10, 12-13, 15, 20, 22-23, 26, 29-30, 32-33, 36-37, 40-41, 43, 65-66, 77, 79-81, 83-85, 94, 100-102, 109-113, 121-123, 131-141
Bracket Airport (LaVerne) CA   p.136
Bremerton WA   p.66-67, 71-73
Chehalis (Centralia) WA   p.100-101, 106-17, 109, 140-141, 146
Friday Harbor WA   p.25-27, 29, 32, 34, 44, 138
Hoquiam WA   p.73, 124-125
Kelso-Longview WA   p.100-101, 106
Lopez Island WA   p.26, 35, 43-44
Monterey CA   p.130
Nanaimo BC   p.53, 56, 63
Newport OR   p.92-94, 96-98, 141, 143-145
North Bend (Southwest Regional) OR   p.129-130
Oceano (Pismo Beach) CA   p.130
Ocean Shores WA   p.66, 73-75, 77, 124-125, 129
Olympia WA   p.94, 101, 124, 146
Orcas Island (Eastsound) WA   p.30, 32, 35, 41-42, 89-90
Port Angeles (Fairchild) WA   p.131, 138
Port Townsend (Jefferson County) WA   p.14-15, 91, 94, 101
Powell River BC   p.19, 43, 56, 57, 61, 63, 65, 131,
Roche Harbor WA   p.27
Santa Ynez CA   p.93
Scappoose OR   p.99-103
Seattle-Tacoma (SeaTac) WA   p.67
Siletz Bay (GlenEden Beach) OR   p.62, 94, 100, 121-126, 130, 140-145

Airport Index

Skagit Regional (Burlington) WA   p.40-42, 131, 133-134
Tillamook OR   p.125-126
Toledo WA   p.140
Whidbey Naval Air Station   p.23, 25, 66-67, 102, 113, 138, 143

Coastal British Columbia Stories
A Regional Series of Books by Wayne J. Lutz

Order at:
www.PowellRiverBooks.com

Coastal BC Living Blog
PowellRiverBooks.blogspot.com

www.ingramcontent.com/pod-product-compliance
Lightning Source LLC
Chambersburg PA
CBHW071734080526
44588CB00013B/2031